Teacher's Guide to
Geography

• Key subject knowledge • Background information • Teaching tips •

SCHOLASTIC

Book End, Range Road, Witney, Oxfordshire, OX29 0YD
www.scholastic.co.uk
© 2012 Scholastic Ltd
1 2 3 4 5 6 7 8 9   2 3 4 5 6 7 8 9 0 1

British Library Cataloguing-in-Publication Data
A catalogue record for this book is available from the
British Library.

ISBN 978 -1407-12778-1
Printed and bound by CPI Group (UK) Ltd, Croydon,
CR0 4YY

Due to the nature of the web, we cannot guarantee
the content or links of any site mentioned. We strongly
recommend that teachers check websites before using
them in the classroom.

Author
John Halocha

Commissioning Editor
Paul Naish

Development Editor
Pollyanna Poulter

Proofreader
Kate Manson

Indexer
Penny Brown

Illustrations
Garry Davies
Hard Lines
Stephen Lillie

Icons
Tomek.gr

Series Designers
Shelley Best and Sarah Garbett

Acknowledgements
The publishers gratefully acknowledge permission
to reproduce the following copyright material:

The National Curriculum for England 2000 © The
Queen's Printer and Controller of HMSO. Reproduced
under the terms of HMSO Guidance Note 8.

An extract from *Primary Geography Handbook
2010* edited by Scoffham, S. © Sheffield:
Geographical Association.

Every effort has been made to trace copyright
holders for the works reproduced in this book,
and the publishers apologise for any inadvertent
omissions.

About the author
John Halocha taught in primary and middle schools
for 18 years and was deputy head teacher in two
schools. In 1991 he moved into teacher education
at Westminster College Oxford, before joining the
University of Durham School of Education in 1996.
He then became Reader in Geography Education
at Bishop Grosseteste University College Lincoln
and retired in the summer of 2012. During his
career he published many journal articles and book
chapters in addition to writing a number of books
on geographical education and primary teaching.
He was President of the Geographical Association
in 2009–2010.

Contents

Introduction 5

Chapter 1 Geographical enquiry and skills 8

Chapter 2 Places 40

Chapter 3 Patterns and processes 71

Chapter 4 Environmental change and sustainable development 110

Chapter 5 Water 133

Chapter 6 Fieldwork 160

Glossary 184

Index 189

Icon key

Information within this book is highlighted in the margins by a series of different icons. They are:

Subject facts
Key subject knowledge is clearly presented and explained in this section.

Why you need to know these facts
Provides justification for understanding the facts that have been explained in the previous section.

Vocabulary
A list of key words, terms and language relevant to the preceding section. Most entries appear in the glossary.

Common misconceptions
Identifies and corrects some of the common misconceptions and beliefs that may be held about the subject area.

Handy tips
Specific tips or guidance on best practice in the classroom.

Golden rules
Core subject concepts which are required to fully understand a subject area.

Amazing facts
Interesting snippets of background knowledge to share.

Questions
Identifies common questions and provides advice on how to answer them.

Teaching ideas
Outlines practical teaching suggestions using the knowledge explained in the preceding section.

Geography

What is a primary geography teacher?

A professional geographer and a primary geography teacher are rather different people. Professional geographers set out to answer questions about how the world is changing. They are interested in understanding the changes happening in the physical and human world: Why is the population increasing more quickly in some countries than in others? How can we predict when volcanoes will erupt and when earthquakes will occur? Primary geography teachers are interested in introducing young people to the huge range of people, places and events in our world. They encourage children to ask questions about both the places they know and places further away. They want them to try to explain why things happen in our world: Why have some people destroyed a **field** to build more houses? Does it matter if we ignore how much energy we use in our home every day? What might happen if we don't change some of the ways in which we live on our planet?

Teaching primary geography is not teaching facts about the world. It's not even teaching children how to find facts, although that is a part of it. It's mainly about helping children to ask geographical questions. This is called geographical enquiry. The children's questions will help them to understand the world. All of your pupils come to school with lots of experiences about the world. They know how to get to the sweet shop from home. They know which streets to go down to avoid large dogs. They hear grown-ups talking about the Earth getting hotter and wonder what the world will be like in their future.

Teaching primary geography is about introducing children to cause and effect: If we burn lots of coal in our power stations, it will affect the **forests** in other countries. In primary geography, children are introduced to the wonderful variety of patterns and processes we find on our planet. They can look at the way in which waves make patterns in the sand on a beach and ask what happens if they put big pebbles in the way. They can look at old maps and photographs of their town and see how the process of urban growth has changed the environment forever. They can think about what their world might be like when they are older. Finding out about people in other places can help children develop a greater awareness of the variety of cultures, values, beliefs and ways of life in different parts of the world. In a world closely linked through travel and communication technologies, these are essential skills for the children's future.

How can this book help?

Having taught primary geography in primary schools, initial teacher education and continuing professional development over the last 36 years, I have seen geography rise from a rarely taught subject during the 1970s, through the early 1990s following its inclusion in the 1991 National Curriculum, and into the new millenium, with all of the modern applications that implies. Recent emphasis on literacy and numeracy saw its decline, but it is now a statutory Foundation subject.

Many primary school teachers have not studied geography beyond GCSE. Many teachers feel that they do not have the knowledge or confidence about the subject to teach geography to their primary classes. This book aims to restore your confidence and interest in geography. It does not aim to provide all the subject facts you will ever need – the world is rather too big, and changing too fast, for that!

This book will give you a clear framework that explains what primary geography is all about. You, as a teacher, will be responsible for selecting the precise content of your geography curriculum, both within your classroom, and in the wider context of contributing towards your school's curriculum. Any curriculum or scheme of work you follow should provide a framework into which you build content and experiences.

This book will provide you with the understanding and ideas necessary to provide a curriculum that is relevant to your pupils within the prescribed legal framework. The resources section at the end of each chapter will give you suggestions for useful hooks on which to hang further, more detailed knowledge and contacts.

The structure of this book

The chapter headings in this book are based on a logical progression through a typical primary geography curriculum.

● Chapter 1 looks at the essentials of primary geography. It explains what geographical enquiry is. It gives examples of how you can plan interesting and relevant enquiries with your pupils. It explains how enquiry should be carried out for Key Stages 1 and 2.

● Chapter 2 focuses on localities. These are the building blocks of effective primary geography. It looks at your school locality and explains how you can find out about it and make the most of what it has to offer. It considers places further afield in Britain, and suggestions are given for finding out about places around the world, using a range of resources to teach about them.

● Chapter 3 explains what geographical patterns and processes are. Examples are provided to help illustrate key points.

● Chapter 4 provides facts and ideas about environmental change and **sustainable development**. It provides the knowledge you need to teach these concepts in primary school. It discusses some of the values implicit in teaching ideas that may be controversial or not yet fully understood by 'experts' in the field.

● Chapter 5 examines the theme of water in geographical contexts. Rivers and coastlines are explained in simple terms. Examples are provided of how to teach children the knowledge and understanding required about rivers and coastlines.

● Chapter 6 explains why fieldwork is important in primary geography. It also provides information on health and safety issues. Three case studies show how progression and continuity can be planned into fieldwork activities throughout the primary age range.

Approaches to teaching and learning

Throughout this book, the emphasis is on active learning and problem-solving. It encourages full use of easily found geographical resources and explains how you can find these in the real world. The world is changing rapidly and knowing facts is not enough. Children need to develop the skills necessary to ask the right questions at the right time. Good primary geography teaching will help them learn to do this. Our planet is a fascinating, varied, but fragile place.

Chapter I

Geographical enquiry and skills

As adults, we use geographical enquiry in many of our day-to-day activities, although we may not always realise it: we look out of the window to see what the **weather** might be like; we plan the best route around the supermarket so we don't have to retrace our steps. We ask questions about the world and try to find ways of answering them, using our previous knowledge. As teachers, we need to think how we can lead children to make enquiries about the world to help them to understand it better.

Geographical enquiry

Subject facts

Geographical enquiry is a process or a sequence and within it is a range of skills. These skills can be developed and will vary depending on the complexity of the enquiry question.

There are seven sequential stages in the process of geographical enquiry:

1. *being aware* of the present knowledge and understanding children have
2. *asking a key question* and perhaps a series of more focused questions
3. *collecting data and evidence* from primary and/or secondary sources
4. *analysing and interpreting* our findings
5. *presenting* what we have found out
6. *making decisions/coming to conclusions*
7. *evaluating* the enquiry.

Key question: What is the best route around the supermarket?

1. **Present knowledge and understanding.** You have been to the supermarket before and know the overall layout. You know where your most frequently bought products are kept. You know there are some sections you never visit. Some parts of the store feel interesting or pleasant to be in.

2. **Key question.** Based on your current needs, you now ask the key question *What is the best route around the supermarket?* This can be supported by more focused questions, such as *Has the layout changed since my last visit? Are there any promotions I want to look at?*

3. **Collecting data.** You look at your shopping list to decide where you need to go. You see some special-offer posters in the window on your way in. You collect a new store layout plan from the front of the shop. You decide how much time you have for your visit.

4. **Analysing and interpreting findings.** At the end of your trip, you draw conclusions on how successful it was. How will you improve the route next time you shop there? What places can be avoided? Did you spend too long browsing in some sections?

5. **Presenting what you found.** You are unlikely to do this formally! However, your experiences may influence how you set out your shopping list next time. You may warn another member of the family about something you experienced.

6. **Making decisions and coming to conclusions.** This is where you decide how you will tackle your next visit. In other words, you use what you found in your enquiry to make changes in the future.

7. **Evaluating the enquiry.** Did you collect all the information you need to improve your next visit? Are there some things you can never predict? (Stores do like to change sections around!) Was it such a bad experience that you will never go there again?

Although this is an example from adult life, it demonstrates how we can tackle geographical questions in a structured way. This was a geographical enquiry because we were dealing with objects in space, routes and the relationship between things: it's a spatial problem and that's what geographers are interested in. It even includes some thoughts about the future because we don't know whether the store will have the same layout next time we visit – just like the world in general: it's always changing and we need to be able to see, and adapt to, those changes.

The shopping example included three key features of geographical enquiry. It was *active* because the shopper was thinking about his or her experiences and adapting his or her behaviour. *Learning* was taking place because information was being used to improve knowledge and understanding of the world. Finally, everything was part of a *process* of linked stages. Effective geographical enquiries help to give children the skills they need in order to think about the world and what is happening in it. This is what primary geography is all about. Geographical enquiry helps children to learn in an active way. Passive teaching methods may pass on geographical information, but children's understanding will be limited. Even so, it is still important to plan enquiries carefully by choosing a focus that is relevant to children. This can also help to build citizenship and personal involvement into the curriculum.

Why you need to know these facts

Good teaching practice in geography at KS1 and KS2 should ensure that children develop knowledge and understanding of places, patterns and processes, as well as environmental change and sustainable development. Suitable geographical skills and methods of enquiry should consistently be used to achieve this.

In other words, we need to help children to ask questions and search for answers about what is happening in the world.

Vocabulary

Key question – a precisely worded question used to start an enquiry. The more carefully it is worded, the more opportunities it will give for understanding. For example, we might ask *Which parts of the road near school are safe and which are dangerous?* when linking geographical work to road safety and citizenship. That will probably generate some factual information. If we ask *Why* are some parts safe and some more dangerous? this leads children to look for reasons as to why things are as they are.

A good key question begs more questions for children to investigate. In the example above, further questions might include:
● How can the safety of the whole street be improved?
● Who should make these improvements and who decides what happens?
● Are improvements better for everyone in our **community** or are some groups left out?

Focused geographical enquiry – happens when a key question is used to solve a geographical problem. It takes the key question and uses the seven enquiry stages (outlined on page 9) to find some answers.

Common misconceptions

Enquiries do not have to ask 'difficult' questions or be complicated. Often, it's the simplest, but most carefully worded, question that leads to a good enquiry.

Handy tip

Get to know your school's geography programme of study and scheme of work for KS1 and KS2. When you come to devise your key question, you can plan the knowledge, skills and understanding the children will experience as they seek answers to it. Additional questions will help you to focus more precisely. The following 'Barnaby Bear' example shows how this works.

Teaching ideas

Using a teaching device

At KS1, you could use Barnaby Bear to ask a key question. A child is to take Barnaby on holiday and the key question could be *Where is Barnaby going?* but this on its own leads to limited chances for enquiry. If we add *and what is it like where Barnaby is going?* this encourages further questions: *Where is it? How will he get there? What's the weather like? What will he do?* You can then start with what children already know about that place and build up your enquiry. It can be made meaningful by helping Barnaby to pack suitable clothes, deciding what he might eat when he gets there and planning some things he will do. Such an enquiry is based on the children's understanding of going on holiday. It starts with the children's own experiences, which makes it easy for them to identify with the geographical enquiry and understand that there is a reason for finding answers to the questions.

Using local resources

At KS2, an enquiry into local street names could be developed. A road near to the school may be called Station Lane, but you can't see a railway station in use today: it's now a builder's merchants. Encourage the children to look carefully at street names and guide them into asking why it's called Station Lane when there seems to be no station there. *What happened to the station?* would be an excellent geographical enquiry, looking closely at changing **land use** and demands for types of **transport**. Children could undertake research using a range of maps, old photographs and interviews with local residents. They could take the investigation into the future by asking what may happen to the station site and what they would like to happen. This introduces futures education and citizenship into geography.

Developing geographical language

Subject facts

Geographical vocabulary uses many everyday words and other more specialised ones. Children increase the range of their vocabulary and confidence if we give them real-world situations in which to practise. For example, if they are writing down a set of directions for a visitor to find their school, they will need to use sequencing words, such as *when* and *next*. They will need to use describing words such as the <u>*tall*</u> *library building*. Also, they will use positional words, such as <u>*next to*</u> *the museum*. Landscape vocabulary may also be useful: *The school is at the top of the hill.*

Geographical vocabulary sometimes fits into hierarchies rather like Russian dolls nesting together. KS1 children should experience this with writing addresses: your name, house number, street, town, county, postcode, country, and of course some children enjoy taking this to the ends of the universe! Vocabulary used like this can help give a sense of scale and pattern.

Geographical vocabulary can be grouped under various headings:

● *Positional vocabulary.* We use this to describe the location of features. It includes words and phrases such as *here, there, up, left, right, behind, in front of, beyond, adjacent, opposite, next to, to the right of, horizon, foreground, background*. It helps us to describe the landscape as well as assisting in giving instructions and finding our way around. This group would also include the main **points of the compass**: north, south, east, west and the many sub-divisions available, such as south-west.

● *Landscape vocabulary.* These are specific words we use for features in the landscape. They can be grouped together depending on the features we are looking at. For example, a list of words linked with rivers would include *valley, stream, basin, meander, tributary, flow,* **erosion**, *estuary, delta, load, waterfall, ford*. There are sets of words specifically for other geographical features such as *settlements, weather, rocks, glacial processes, coastlines*. These are explained in the relevant chapters later.

● *Data-collecting vocabulary.* We use this when we are collecting information about people and places. Examples include *temperature, water flow, windspeed, traffic flow, rainfall, pollution levels, degrees, kilometres* and so on.

Many other words have geographical uses. The terms *transport*, **industry**, *tourism*, **migration**, *global warming* and so on all help to describe and explain the world. Other chapters in this book will explain in more depth the vocabulary you need.

Why you need to know these facts

By providing real opportunities for children to use and understand a growing range of words and phrases, you will be helping them to build more detailed models of the world in their minds. It will also be a chance to learn how flexible various words can be. For example: the River Amazon and the River Severn are both rivers, but they vary hugely in size and in the processes and geographical issues surrounding them; a **refugee** may be someone who has made a conscious decision to leave their homeland or they may have been forced out by other people.

Common misconceptions

● Misconceptions can happen in geography when stereotypes develop. Children, and indeed others they meet in their community, may have a picture of an 'African' person. By studying people in other countries we can begin to give children alternative pictures and vocabulary about the world. Thus they may adapt their list from *poor* and *starving* by adding *proud, strong sense of community* and *hard-working*.

● Misconceptions also occur with the physical world: *You don't get snow at the equator because it's too hot.* You do! It depends on the *altitude* of the land and the **climate** zones (further vocabulary to develop children's more flexible understanding of the world).

Teaching ideas

- At KS1, build groups of related geographical words with the children. When studying built-up places, for example, the vocabulary might include *house*, **factory**, *bank*, *shop*, *flats*, *police station*, *supermarket*. Words related to the seaside include *beach*, *sand*, *cliffs*, *pier*, *shore*, *rockpools*, **tide**, *waves*.
- Some lists of geographical words can be linked in a hierarchy. Get the children to sort these and perhaps link them to features on photographs. For example, when looking at settlements, the list would include *house*, **hamlet**, **village**, *town*, *city*, **conurbation**.
- Discussion about the children's addresses will reveal how places are 'nested' one inside the other: house name or number, street name, place name, county, postcode, country.
- Relate vocabulary to the real world. Stand at the front of a line of children and go on a geography word walk. As you say each phrase, get the child behind you to whisper it to the next child, and so on down the line, for example: *We're walking <u>down</u> the corridor, going <u>through</u> the door, <u>across</u> the playground, <u>up</u> the slope, <u>around</u> the corner…*

Asking geographical questions

Subject facts

You may have noticed that the enquiry questions we ask can vary. Good planning will include a range of questions. The key questions need to help children to understand their world and not just learn facts. *What shops are there on the high street?* would probably lead to a factual, information-collecting approach. *What type of shop does our community think should be opened in the derelict building on the high street?* will open up a whole range of further enquiry questions. *Which shops are used most? What new shops do people want and why? Where is the nearest similar facility?* and so on. These questions will demand that children use a range of geographical skills to find the answers and actually take part in the learning process.

At KS1, a study of the school grounds might use these questions:
- What grows in the grounds?
- Where does it grow?
- Why is there a lot of litter on the playground?
- Where does the water go when it rains?

Make sure that the children learn to use a range of questions. Sometimes, closed questions are useful, such as *Where is Kenya?* This helps to develop children's locational knowledge. However, to develop real understanding of the world, children also need to extend their use of a range of open questions, such as *Why do so many lorries use the road outside school? How can we make crossing that road safer? Where would the best place be to site a new pedestrian crossing and why?*

Good enquiry questions can be about different things. Some focus on places: *What is it like to be a child living in St Lucia?* Others look at change and processes: *How is the coast near Hunstanton changing?* Issues also raise relevant questions: *Do we really need a bypass to our town?* Finally, questions can test a hypothesis: *If we put litter bins in carefully chosen places, will we get less litter blowing into our school grounds?*

Active enquiry uses questions set by both you and your children. You will have to decide on the best balance. Your decision will depend on your learning objectives. *Who shops in the high street?* helps to establish existing knowledge. *How can we find out what new shops people want?* helps children to think about the best way to collect information.

For many years, geographers have used five basic questions on which to build their enquiries:
- What is this place like?
- Why is this place as it is?
- How is this place connected to other places?
- How is this place changing?
- What would it feel like to be in this place?

These are well-established broad geographical questions. Geographers ask them to help explain what is happening on our planet. More and more, geographers are being asked to help in predicting what may happen in the future, using the information they collect and analyse. Our work with young children aims to provide a framework for them to begin to think spatially about the world in which they live. Many organisations today ask geographers to help them solve questions. *What effect might* a new shopping centre have on existing town centres in a 50-mile radius? Where might future global flashpoints occur as more and more people place demands on the global reserves of fresh water? What effect might changes in the gender balance of a working population have on demands for social services within a region? You might think that these are not questions for KS1 or KS2, but they do show how geographical questions have a range of scales and emphasise the importance of cause and effect, patterns and processes.

Why you need to know these facts

In the late 1980s, Her Majesty's Inspectors were concerned that very few primary teachers understood what geography really is. They found little evidence to show that geographical work was carefully planned and structured. Links with other subjects were often vague, partly as a result of teachers using topic webs for planning. Amendments were subsequently made in order to ensure that children experienced a geography curriculum that really did focus on geographical aims and concepts. That's why enquiry based on asking geographical questions is central.

Vocabulary

When you are devising your enquiry questions, choose simple, clear vocabulary. Keep questions short and match them to the key stage of children.

Questions starting with *What* sometimes lead only to factual work. For example, *What will Barnaby use to travel to…?* may be appropriate at KS1 because it will lead children to investigate various types of transport and develop their vocabulary and thoughts about the best transport to use. At KS2, the question *Why might it be better to travel by…?* encourages children to justify why one type of transport may be better than another – it draws on their factual knowledge and asks them to demonstrate an understanding about appropriate types of transport. Ask questions that lead to explanations: *How… What… Why… Can we…?*

Common misconceptions

Sometimes, the questions asked are far too complex for primary school children. A good question does not have to be long or difficult. The real skill is to find one that ensures that children extend their geographical skills and understanding.

Teaching ideas

Working together

When planning, try to ensure as often as possible that both you and the children devise the questions. If they all come from you, children may feel less ownership of the work they are doing.

Ideally, a school geography co-ordinator will have a whole-school view of the range of questions that children will experience as they progress through the school. Before you begin planning your questions, talk to the co-ordinator to see how your questions will build on his or her previous experiences.

Also, the sign of an effective geographer is to be able to create questions for which the answers really do help to explain your own world. This is one of the broader aims of primary school geography.

Observing, collecting and recording data and evidence

Subject facts

Geographical evidence and data can be collected from many sources. The key word here is *appropriate*. At KS1, children should observe and record geographical information. As you gain experience, you will learn how to help children choose the best way of collecting and recording evidence to solve the question or questions they are asking. Sometimes they will ask the wrong question, but you can use this as an active teaching point. Broadly speaking, appropriate sources can be grouped into the following:

Observation

An excellent starting point is first-hand observation in the real world. Children need to learn to observe really carefully and not to look just in general terms. A real skill here is to help them link what they already know with what they see in a scene that is new to them. For example, they have looked at their local stream and are now on a residential visit in another part of the country: good teaching will help children to use what they know about flowing water and apply it on a bigger scale.

Good observation is closely linked to asking the right questions: *Why do most people in this place travel to work by cycle?* This will tell us much more about the place than *How many cycles, cars and buses use the road in an hour?* The answer to the first question gives us real geographical evidence.

Atlases, maps and globes

Atlases, maps, globes, sketches and online resources such as Google Maps® give us various types of evidence. One of the skills is choosing the one that is right for the job and that matches the age and ability of the children.

Children need to use a wide range of maps and plans. The **scales** should vary according to the experience of the children and the type of work being done. A large-scale plan might show the top of their table or the layout of their classroom. Smaller-scale maps and plans show a greater area, such as the whole school or the locality.

Commercially available maps often state their scale as a ratio. A large-scale map of your local area might be at a scale of 1:1250. This scale of map is useful with primary children because individual buildings, fences and local names can be clearly seen. A 1:50,000 scale map shows a much greater area. However, to do this, much more use is made of **symbols** and a lot more detail is shown. This can be confusing for primary children.

When you decide to use a globe, atlas or map with your children, be clear about two things. First, is it the most suitable resource to use for the point you wish them to understand? For instance, there is little point in using a globe to locate London and Lincoln. Second, be clear about the geographical skills that children can learn and apply when using various resources. A globe can be used to develop a three-dimensional view of the world. It can help to explain vocabulary such as **hemisphere**, **equator**, *polar regions*, and the relationships between them. An atlas requires a knowledge of what maps can show: some contain physical features while others have information about human activities. Also, alphabetical and numerical skills can be taught and reinforced when using an atlas to find information.

People

People can provide evidence. We can observe them carefully in their place, and record what they do. We can ask them questions and collect data from them. We can ask them how they feel about places. People can be invited into school to work with children. A local environmentalist might discuss changes to wildlife in the area. A school governor could talk about life in a distant locality in which they have lived, as could some of the children in your class if they have lived in other places.

Artefacts

Artefacts give us useful information. Restaurant menus can tell us about local produce, traditions and lifestyles if we ask the right questions. For example, *Why is there a lot of fish on the menu from our partner school in Portugal?* This well-chosen key question will lead to enquiry into the position of the restaurant, the climate and what happens nearby, at the seaside. At KS1, hats from around the world make an excellent focus for looking at climate, jobs and other ways of life. Comparing children's toys can help to explain how technology is used in other countries.

Equipment

Equipment gives us geographical evidence: a weather station records patterns and changes; a digital video camera can be used to speed up patterns in the environment; websites can be accessed and compared; oranges floating along a river help us to work out the speed and direction of the flow (this is a cheap and easily seen item that floats and is disposable!).

Other secondary sources

We have to use secondary sources in geography because it is impossible to visit everywhere. By using secondary sources we can learn that all of them are selective and only give us a part of the picture. We can compare sources and learn to choose the particular ones that have the information we need.

Careful study of secondary sources adds to our evidence. Photographs, stories, songs, beliefs and news reports are just a few we can use. Keep an eye on national and international news websites for up-to-date footage from around the world. Short clips can be shown in class, alongside relevant resources, such as an inflatable globe, or Google Earth®. (Always check that the content of a website is appropriate before showing it to your class.) A discussion of what is happening around the world will develop children's locational knowledge and their interest in other people and places.

Recording

Geographers record their observations in many ways. Field sketches, photographs, interviews, maps and plans, graphs and digital recording are just a few of them. Again, the real skill is in choosing a recording method that makes the observation clear and lets you analyse it easily.

Drawing maps and plans helps children to understand what they are used for and how to represent the real world in symbolic form. Children learn to decide what they want to show. They begin to adapt scale and proportion. They learn to use symbols and create **keys**. **Grid references** help them to locate places on their maps and plans. Maps and plans can also be used to record evidence. Choosing words and names to add to their plans puts geographical vocabulary into practice. The results can also tell you something about children's level of understanding and aid your pupil assessment programme.

Field sketches are drawings made while out on fieldwork. They are not intended to show everything in a view, but are selective. For instance, a field sketch might record land use – **crops**, woodland and moorland.

Why you need to know these facts

Information about the world can be collected from many sources. Textbooks and worksheets have only a small part to play. If you use a wide range of resources when children are observing and collecting information, they will be more interested and have the chance to develop a wider range of skills. This includes the important skill of comparing information and deciding what is most useful and accurate.

Vocabulary

Vocabulary linked to globes includes:

Axis – an imaginary line through the Earth connecting the north and south poles, around which the Earth moves.

Continent – the seven large areas of land on the Earth.

Crop – food (eg wheat) and non-food (eg oilseed rape) plants grown, for sale, in fields.

Equator – an imaginary line drawn around the middle of the Earth.

Greenwich meridian – an imaginary line of longitude, drawn from the north to the south pole, which passes through Greenwich in London.

Hemisphere – the northern hemisphere is all the surface of the Earth north of the equator; the southern hemisphere is all the surface south of the equator.

Latitude – the angular distance of a place north or south of the equator.

Longitude – the angular distance of a place east or west of the Greenwich meridian.

North and south poles – imaginary points around which the Earth spins.

The tropics – parts of the Earth's surface up to 23°27' north and south of the equator.

The main words used when working with maps and plans are:

Grid references – most maps and plans have a grid of fine lines, breaking up the land into a series of squares.

Map-makers provide two main ways to use grid references and it's important that children understand both. One method puts the letters or numbers between the grid lines (see Figure 1). We read off the horizontal line first and then the vertical. So, the grid reference for the church will be 2C. This reference is talking about the whole of the square of land at 2C. This method of grid referencing is often used on town street plans.

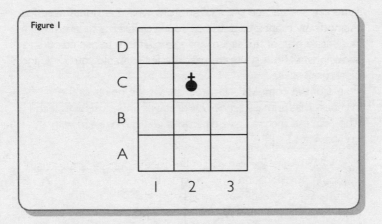

Figure 1

The other type of grid reference uses lines with numbers at the end of each line (see Figure 2). This method allows us to locate an exact point on the map. The user needs to understand that the distance between each line is divided into ten equal lengths.

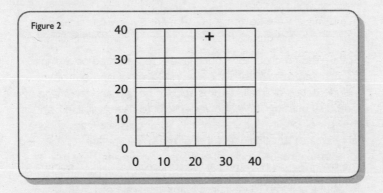

Figure 2

So, to give the grid reference for this church, we read across the horizontal line to line 20 and then estimate how many tenths we have to move to the right to locate the church. In this case it is halfway, so the first part of the grid reference is 205. We then read up the vertical line and find the line below the church (30). We estimate how many tenths further up the church is located and find it to be 8. The second half of the grid reference is 308. The full grid reference for the church is 205308.

Key – a key will contain all the symbols used on a plan or map to explain what they mean.

Land use – maps and plans often show what the land is used for. A good way to introduce this to young children is to give them a large-scale plan of the classroom and ask them to use colours to show what various parts are used for, for example your desk and cloakroom space.

Points of the compass – Figure 3 shows the points of the compass that primary school children will find it useful to learn. They can use them to give directions and can be used with a compass at KS2.

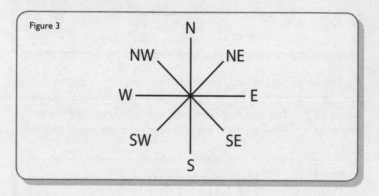

Figure 3

Scale – this controls how much land is represented on a plan or map. Large-scale plans show a small area of land, but often include details of small features, such as hedges and the shape of individual buildings. It will be very useful to have available plans of the school locality at a scale of 1:1250. Small-scale maps show a large area of land. Main features of the landscape are represented, for example roads, blocks of buildings and **woods**. They rely heavily on symbols to represent features and can be rather hard for young children to interpret. Maps at a scale of 1:50,000 are small-scale maps.

Symbols – these are used on maps and plans to represent features in the landscape. They are a shorthand code used by map-makers because maps would look very confusing if every feature was drawn as it looked in real life. Churches may be shown by a + and woods by an area of green with just two or three simple tree shapes within it. Colours can be used to make symbols clearer and more useful. Various types of road can be shown in different colours: motorways are often blue, while country lanes may be yellow.

Handy tip

The key skills to using atlases are:
- Choose the right atlas for the job.
- Remember that pages may focus on physical or human features. Also, they may tackle a theme such as farming.
- Use the contents page correctly.
- Know how to use the index. This has many sub-skills: page numbers, grid references, **latitude** and **longitude**, alphabetical order.
- Be aware of the overall layout of the atlas.
- Know relevant vocabulary, for example *equator, northern* and *southern hemispheres,* **continents**.
- Think creatively. This will help you to find resources that are effective, and that may be free of charge.

If you want to use a piece of equipment but don't have it in school, try:
- the geography department in your local secondary school
- the county geography/humanities inspector
- a teachers' resource centre
- parents and governors
- local industry.

Golden rules

- Be aware of the range of sources you use. If you only use travel brochures when studying another country, children will get only a small picture of the place.
- Check up on the age of the resource. Use older ones if changes and the past are important, otherwise keep as up-to-date as you can.

Teaching ideas

Collecting evidence
Choose evidence-collecting methods that give interesting and relevant data. For instance, if you want to see how time changes

things, set up a digital video camera to record four hours of change as a trickle of water flows across your sand-tray river model (see Figure 17 on page 144). Children will learn things from the video that they would not be able to see from first-hand observation. It's also an example of using evidence that is time-effective in a busy school day and of applying ICT to solving a geographical problem.

Using ICT

Use a paint package to draw maps and plans. There are special map-drawing packages available too. The advantages of using a computer are:

- Mistakes can be removed and changes made easily.
- Colours, lines and shading are readily available, which allows children to spend more time developing geographical thinking than colouring skills.
- Size, position and proportion can easily be shown using features such as shape tools.

Analysing evidence and drawing conclusions

Subject facts

Facts alone are not enough. Children could learn the population of the ten biggest cities in England, but this would not tell them much about why they are the biggest. Geographers analyse information to help to explain the world. For example, analysing employment figures from the ten fastest growing towns or cities may provide clues about the growth of particular industries. Data from towns with declining populations could add much to this picture. From there, we can try to draw conclusions: Why are these processes happening? Can we do anything to change them or, indeed, should we? Thinking about the rapid population growth in the south-east of England alongside minimal economic growth in the north-east helps to show the reality of many geographical questions. It may also help to explain why we need to come to conclusions. Analysing data also helps us to understand how complex the world is: people may not like spending hours in traffic jams and living in 'over-priced' properties, but thousands do. This then raises further enquiry questions and so geographers go on learning more about the world.

Children will develop as primary geographers as you give them opportunities to observe, record, analyse and finally come to conclusions about the world.

Why you need to know these facts

Geographical information can be very powerful. Link this with new forms of technology and consider the world in which children will live. They will have access to huge amounts of information from many cultures. They will need the skills of analysis in order to draw conclusions. These will affect their lives and those of other people. Is it unsafe to travel to that country for a holiday or is the media creating a negative image? If enough tourists go to that country, will it become a safer place to visit because greater income changes people's lives? Again, this is quite a complex example, but is used to show why we need effective skills in analysing evidence and drawing conclusions.

Common misconceptions

It can be tempting to come to only one conclusion to keep things simple. A key skill in helping children to draw conclusions is to accept that there may not be one 'right' answer. This allows them the chance to rank a range of ideas in order of preference by thinking about where their information came from and what they did with it.

Teaching ideas

Developing an enquiry
Different groups of children can develop an enquiry, and then compare ideas and conclusions. For example, groups could work on design layouts for a new school garden area. They would have

to think about land use, the needs of various people, money factors, how it will look and ease of looking after it. After their enquiry and presenting their findings, children may also learn that many decisions are a compromise. This type of enquiry can therefore support a citizenship dimension within the curriculum.

Using local knowledge

Keep in touch with what is happening in the school locality. Events and changes can often be the start of an interesting and relevant enquiry. At KS1, the opening of a new baker's shop near the school might lead to a visit and to developing answers to some of these enquiry questions:

- Why did they decide to open the shop?
- What do they sell?
- Where do the bread and cake ingredients come from?
- Which bread and cake recipes come from other countries?

A tasting session will be enjoyable and extend children's experiences of foods from around the world.

At KS2, perhaps a school governor or a parent is planning to visit India as part of their work. You study a village in India and work with children to develop questions they might collect information on during the visit. This could be compared to other sources of information that children find in books, on the web and in locality packs. Perhaps they could keep in contact by email while the governor or parent is away in India.

Identifying and explaining different views

Subject facts

People around the world hold different views on many issues. The following examples are intended to start you thinking geographically! In this way, you may begin to see how daily events can form the basis of primary geographical work.

- Planners and politicians currently hold a range of views about the development of housing estates and **new towns** in the south-east of England. These may not coincide with views held by environmentalists and farmers. The people who either wish to or have to live in that region may hold another set of views. Try to find issues in the localities studied by your children about which different people have various points of view.

● Farmers in some African countries decide to supply European supermarkets with specialist vegetables that command high prices. They stop growing the produce needed locally. Agriculturalists and environmentalists make suggestions on the long-term effects this may have on soils and people's diets in those countries. Supermarkets need all-year access to produce, which means approaching countries with suitable climates. European **consumers** watch television cookery programmes using this produce and want to recreate the recipes for themselves regardless of seasonal change and natural cycles.

These two examples demonstrate other facts: issues can happen at a range of scales and can be equally important – a noisy playground next to houses is of real concern at a local scale, while the causes and effects of global warming affect nearly everyone; they show the real importance of cause and effect as geographical concepts; they illustrate patterns and processes.

Why you need to know these facts

Geography that is taught using enquiry methods is highly valuable. It exposes children to real-world issues; it challenges assumptions; it requires the ability to see the world from other people's points of view. This will affect the way you and your pupils choose enquiry questions. Children will want to know what you think. They may even want to spend more time on research than the timetable permits! They will need to have access to a range of resources. All this means that you have to be well prepared. However, you can approach geography in a different way from other subjects. You don't have to know everything the children will learn. You don't need to know everything going on in your locality. You *do* need to know how to find out and how to provide appropriate learning experiences. Finally, you need to have thought about your personal style and beliefs when confronting geographical issues alongside your children.

Vocabulary

The following words are presented to help you formulate your own views on developing geographical issues. What do they mean for you as a teacher?

Attitudes – how do children approach learning about other people and places?

Background – what information, ideas, experiences, questions and skills do children bring with them to school?

Balance – the need to ensure children experience different points of view.

Bias – do some resources only give one point of view?

Choice – how wide a range of resources do you provide in geography lessons?

Culture – ways of life in different places need to be brought to the classroom.

Indoctrination – we must ensure that children experience a range and balance of ideas, facts, beliefs and values.

Information – geographical information comes from many sources: newspapers, television, books, videos, maps, satellite images and so on.

Perspective – as a whole school, work to ensure that children have opportunities to experience a range of points of view in geography lessons.

Sources – you need to know who supplies the information that children will use.

Values – children need the opportunity to respect and understand values held by other people around the world.

Common misconceptions

Words often have various meanings, and children may be confused between the meaning they bring to school and the ways in which words are used in geography. They may hear people say *What a relief!* and confuse it with the word *relief* we use to describe the shape of the land. (It's also sometimes used to describe how help is given to people in other places.) When we talk about Europe, do we include Britain as a part of

Europe or do we perhaps say *When you go to Europe…* without considering possible misconceptions that children may develop?

Handy tip

In lesson plans, list the key vocabulary you intend to use. Spend a few minutes thinking about your definitions and how you'll use the words with the children.

Teaching ideas

● Develop geography displays that use a wide range of geographical words.
● Provide a range of resources so that children can compare how words and ideas are presented.
● Show short video pieces related to the work you are doing, but turn off the sound. Get groups of children to write what they think the commentary might be and what people on the video are saying.

Presenting information

Subject facts

The enquiry approach to learning and teaching in geography is based on extending our understanding of the world and making it available to other people to interpret and use. *What will the weather be like tomorrow in my home area and where I'm going on holiday?* Weather forecasts, satellite images on a web page and a phone call to your hotel will communicate that information to you in different ways. The television weather forecast will give you facts and offer predictions at a broad scale. The satellite image gives you live data on your computer, but you need to know how to interpret it. The phone call gives you local knowledge.

Involving children in choosing the best way to communicate information for a particular task and audience helps them in two ways. First, they learn the skills needed to select information and communicate it. Second, by doing this they begin to learn the selective and perhaps biased nature of the information. (The wonderfully sunny photographs in that holiday brochure may not be totally true!) Nearly everything is written and presented for a potential audience. We cannot travel everywhere, but new forms of communication sometimes give the impression we can. Much of our information does come from secondary sources. If children become involved in describing and explaining what they find out about other places, they may begin to understand the benefits and limitations of some of the things they read about the wider world. For example, record the weather forecasts for the next day from two different television channels or news websites. Compare the information they give and the locations of where they say various types of weather will happen. Are they identical? The following day, look back to see how accurate they were by using the meteorological office website **www.metoffice.gov.uk** and the weather actually experienced at school.

Children could write directions for getting to school from particular places in the locality and these could then be compared.

Why you need to know these facts

You should approach this section with great confidence! You will probably have been effectively teaching the literacy for some time or have analysed it in depth during your teacher education course. Geographical enquiry and issues can give you excellent, lively and relevant source materials to use within a literacy approach. Here are some examples:

- newspaper articles about change in the locality
- children's fiction containing detailed descriptions of places
- information from **aid** agencies about the needs of people in other countries
- cookery recipes from other countries
- email messages from children in schools linked with your own
- instructions for travelling from one place to another

- messages on holiday postcards
- tourist information leaflets.

   Perhaps the main fact to consider here is the idea that we need to move on from the notion of one subject being used to support another, suggesting that one has greater relevance or importance. Teachers are being encouraged to develop more flexible ways of teaching literacy. Careful use of geographical texts can provide opportunities to have clear literacy goals while using texts to support current geographical work. For example, when studying reports, children might need a range of newspaper versions of an event such as an earthquake. The root of this issue lies in effective planning. English provides a structure of processes and skills. Geography provides real-world questions and personal involvement of children. Together, they can ensure that you cover the requirements of any geography curriculum.

Teaching ideas

Fieldwork reports

Use fieldwork reports as an opportunity to develop accurate descriptive writing. If you have links with a school in another locality, encourage children to write accurate accounts of changes taking place in your school locality to compare with those in another locality.

Fieldwork techniques

Subject facts

Fieldwork is essential in all school geography plans. Chapter 6 looks at this important area in depth. The key facts of fieldwork are:

- It can take place almost anywhere – from the school grounds to a residential visit in another European country.
- Activities can vary across a wide continuum. At one end it's very teacher-directed with a lot of teacher input. At the other end, children design a geographical enquiry, carry it out and reach conclusions under careful adult supervision.

- It may be done in short bursts of time over a long period, for example taking weather measurements each day over a term. Alternatively, it may be four days away in a contrasting locality.
- It provides opportunities to experience the real world. Although some children are able to travel or go on day trips with their families, others have much more limited experiences. Dangers of the modern world can also limit children's opportunities because parents are rightly concerned about letting them wander on their own. Watching and hearing a waterfall in the Lake District can be an amazing experience for some children, while, for others, the chance to explore a multicultural inner-city marketplace could be equally exciting and new. However, these trips do need excellent planning and supervision.

Fieldwork requires careful planning and the highest consideration for safety. If these are present, it can result in some of the most memorable experiences of primary school.

There are many fieldwork techniques and instruments to use. Chapter 6 looks at these in detail.

Why you need to know these facts

Primary teachers are very busy and fieldwork takes time to prepare. Timetables are overcrowded and good fieldwork needs a flexible timetable to accommodate it. It can cost money, which is of course limited in schools. Geography is not a high-profile subject and may not have a strong place in the school philosophy, adequate timetabling slots and other resources. So, teachers who want to do fieldwork must be clear about the advantages for individual children and the school in general.

Golden rules

- Plan fieldwork into your programmes of study at regular intervals. This will help with progress and continuity in children's geographical understanding.
- Be very clear about your aims and objectives. This will help justify the time, money and resources that your fieldwork will need.

- Get influential people involved: a school governor telling others the value of the work they were involved in as a helper will do no harm.
- Be meticulous with planning and health and safety issues.

Decision-making and coming to conclusions

Subject facts

Some geographical events take place without human activity: volcanoes erupt and **hurricanes** travel across the planet. However, many events take place as a result of human activity. Some of this happens without the people involved always being aware of what they are doing. For example, if we pollute the upper course of a river, we may not understand the effects this will have when the polluted water arrives further downstream. Other human activity is a direct result of people making decisions to change or adapt the environment in some way.

Information is needed to make informed decisions. This takes us right back to the enquiry process itself. We ask a question, collect and analyse data and present the findings. These may then be used to inform decision-making. Geographers become involved in many types of decision-making processes. Where, for example, might the route of a new motorway be located to minimise visual, noise and environmental pollution? To answer this today, 3D computer mapping programs are used to model the region and demonstrate how the route would look and the effects it might have. Another enquiry might look at how new coastal defences on a stretch of the east coast might affect the shape of the coastline and the immediate environment. Detailed surveys, analyses of previous projects, discussions with local residents and computer simulations would be used to make decisions.

Use your own knowledge of the local area and the wider world to support children in their enquiries. It is helpful to build up your own bank of examples of how decisions have been made. For example, if a piece of derelict land near the school is being built upon, keep local newspaper reports about it, take photographs and record the views of local people. These resources can then be used at a later time with classes just starting out on an enquiry about changes to land use in the local area.

Why you need to know these facts

If geographical enquiries at school are to be based on real-world issues that children can relate to, the process will give them the opportunity to become actively involved in decision-making skills. For example, by finding out about the real road-safety issues near their school, children could submit proposals for improvements to the council, police and other authorities. This would involve them in citizenship education, both in becoming aware of the democratic decision-making process and in terms of their rights and responsibilities as citizens.

Taking part in decision-making activities also helps children to understand that there are often a number of different sides to any issue. The world is not black and white. Again, this goes back to the key skills of knowing what question to ask, collecting the best information, evaluating it, presenting what has been found and using it to assist in making decisions.

Vocabulary

Enquiry – asking a question about the world and designing a way of answering it.
Decision-making – the process of coming to a conclusion on how to resolve an issue, for example how we decide where to put new seats in the playground.

Questions

Should primary age children really be getting involved in local issues? After all, their enquiries might easily upset local people, a parent or governor.
This question can be answered in two ways:

First, at primary level children should be able to: recognise how people can improve the environment; understand how decisions about places and environments affect the future quality of people's lives; and recognise how and why people may seek to manage environments sustainably and identify opportunities for their own involvement. As geography is a Foundation subject, teachers have a legal requirement to involve their pupils in geographical issues. If teachers feel that they have little scope for freedom in teaching and learning styles in some subjects, geography allows them to help children to ask questions based on real-world experiences.

Second, as teachers, we need to consider the relevance of the school curriculum to children's lives now and in the future. This will involve us in some hard thinking about the type of learning experiences we create. Is it sufficient, for example, to teach children how to read a map and know where St Lucia is? Do we need to introduce them to the exciting and wonderful range of landscapes, events, peoples and values that exist across the world? Do we need to help them to understand how people, places and events around the world are increasingly connected? Should children learn that people have varying lifestyles, ideas, beliefs and values? A flexible school geography curriculum should give primary teachers the opportunity to take control of the content and processes in the learning environment. It is up to teachers to use this freedom creatively and responsibly.

Teaching ideas

Local resources

A lot of your geographical enquiry will take place in your school's locality. Good teaching ideas will arise when you keep a close eye on what is going on around the school:

- Read the local newspapers.
- Watch regional television news.
- Talk to parents, governors and local people.
- Use the local services, such as shops, libraries and banks.
- Talk to your children to find out what they know about the locality and what is important to them.

Resources

Useful reading

Achieving QTS. Teaching Primary Geography by Catling, S. & Willy, T. (Exeter: Learning Matters, 2009).

'Enquiries and investigations' by Dinkele, G., in *Primary Geography Handbook*, edited by Scoffham, S. (Sheffield: Geographical Association, 2010).

'Are there different types of geographical enquiry?' in *Geography 3–11. A guide for teachers* by Cooper, H., Rowley, C. & Asquith, S. (London: Fulton, 2006).

'Using dialogue to engage children with challenging ideas: geography and global citizenship' by Hurford, D., in *Cross-curricular Approaches to Teaching and Learning*, edited by Rowley, C. & Cooper, H. (London: Sage, 2009).

'Focus on Global Learning', *Primary Geographer*, Number 71 (Sheffield: Geographical Association, Spring 2010).

Technically Geography. Lessons combining geography and ICT for Y1/2 by Bowden, D. & Copeland, P. (Sheffield: Geographical Association, 2004).

'Focus on new technologies', *Primary Geographer*, Number 67 (Sheffield: Geographical Association, Autumn 2008).

'Geography and ICT' by Russell, K., in *Primary Geography Handbook*, edited by Scoffham, S. (Sheffield: Geographical Association, 2010).

Teaching resources

Atlases – The school needs a wide range, from infant atlases to at least one complex atlas. Don't buy class sets. They are too expensive and date too quickly.

Globes – There are a number of different types: those showing physical features; those showing human features; those with surfaces that take non-permanent marker pens (they have continent and country outlines and can be used by children in many ways); chalk globes similar to those described above; large inflatable globes that are excellent stimuli for KS1; antique globes that show how people in times past thought the world was.

Maps – Aim to build up a collection of different maps and plans so children can see their many uses. The following is a starting point: the school and its grounds; the locality – your region; the United Kingdom; town plans; shopping centre plans; the London Underground; bus routes; old maps and plans of various places; plans of proposed local developments; tourist information leaflets; maps on stamps and postcards; wrapping-paper maps; playmats; storybooks with maps, for example *The Hobbit* and *Winnie the Pooh*; boardgames and computer games; CD-ROMs.

Photographs – Those taken at ground level; oblique photographs taken from up high and looking down at an angle; vertical aerial photographs looking straight down; satellite images showing either natural colours as seen from space or computer-generated colours that bring out otherwise hidden details.

ICT – There are many useful resources that can be used in geography. Data-handling packages can store, analyse and present information. Word-processing programs can record and present results. Paint and graphics packages to draw maps. Digital cameras for recording fieldwork, both as photos or as time-lapse videos. Specialised robots can be programmed to teach children geographical and spatial vocabulary. Simulations can let children model the world, look at changes and consider the future.
● Websites provide access to a wide range of resources, for example: **www.iecc.org**; **www.oxfam.org.uk/coolplanet/kidsweb**; **www.geography.org.uk/resources/adifferentview**
● Fly to and explore anywhere in the world with Google Earth®.
● Webcams allow environments to be studied at a distance or over periods of time.
● Audio/video recorders are useful for interviews and environmental sounds.
● Overhead projectors and PowerPoint® presentations to communicate geographical findings.

Other resources – DVDs; stories; recipes; information books; diaries; visitors; artefacts, for example rocks, food samples and clothes; radio and television programmes; films; models; newspapers; magazines.

Chapter 2

Places

Geographers study the world at a range of scales. Sometimes they investigate small places, such as a town centre, while at other times they seek to explain events on a global scale, for example, *Will the sea level really rise during the next 30 years?* To deal with this geography uses the words *place* and *locality*.

All *places* have a *location* and a *site*. *Location* means the position of a geographical feature in relation to other features in the landscape. A feature could be a hill, a village, a railway station, a wood, and so on. A village may have grown up near a river, just beyond an area liable to flooding, but close enough for water to be got for humans and animals. Nearby forests may have provided building materials. Settlements sometimes grew up just beyond the walls of Roman forts, which provided both protection and trade possibilities. When children investigate the positions of places and features in the landscape, they are learning to see the links between places.

The *site* is the actual place where the settlement is built. A village may have grown up on land that drains well. Shops were often located at corners and road junctions in 19th century housing areas so that they were easily reached by foot. A piece of woodland may have certain species of plants in it because the site provides the required amounts of sunlight, water, soil and space to grow. The south-facing slopes of some hillsides can make good sites for certain crops, such as vines. The site of a new leisure centre, for example, is the actual area of land on which the leisure centre will be built.

Places and localities

Subject facts

What are places?

Places can vary in shape, size, content and location, depending on what a geographer wishes to study. There is no one set definition of a *place*, simply because it can contain a variety of things. These examples explain this:

● If we are interested in how a village pond is changing and how it might be managed more sustainably, then the place is the pond and its location.

● If we are studying how a large new estate of houses is changing a village, the place is the whole village.

● If we are examining how a river valley is becoming affected by more regular flooding, the place is the river valley.

● If we are studying the effects of tourism on an island in the Mediterranean Sea, then the whole island is the place.

Place is therefore a flexible concept that can cover a wide range of scales. Places don't exist in isolation – they are linked to other places. The water flowing into the pond will affect it. Job opportunities further afield will affect the people living on the new estate. The river valley will be affected by what happens to water on its way to the valley, and by wider weather patterns. Tourism will be affected by global trends in where people want to take holidays.

Geographers today don't study only the physical and human features of a place. They are also interested in explaining it as a 'meeting place' – somewhere where people, ideas, values, building styles and so on have come together and reacted with each other. This is a useful way of studying places as it helps to draw out the idea that places are constantly changing and evolving. This happens largely as a result of the places' connections with other places.

It is also important that children begin to develop a 'sense of place' to help them to know how they feel about somewhere and what it means to them.

What are localities?

The word *locality* has been adopted in order to help teachers choose a manageable area to study. The idea was that it is better to investigate a small area in detail than a large area that requires too much understanding from primary age children.

At KS1:

> the 'locality' of the school is its immediate vicinity, including school buildings and grounds and the surrounding area within easy access. The contrasting locality should be an area of similar size.

At KS2, localities:

> should cover an area larger than the school's immediate vicinity and will normally cover the homes of the majority of pupils in the school.

When we study a locality, we don't have to research every aspect of it. We can pick an issue or theme to study in detail. This is important when planning the whole-school geography curriculum. As children progress, they will need opportunities to study their locality from various perspectives, benefiting from carefully planned continuity.

There are a variety of ways in which progress and continuity can be planned into a study of the school locality. One is to gradually widen the actual content: for example, a study on houses and homes will lead on to work about local services. Another is to gradually extend the locality and investigate further afield: start in the school grounds, then investigate local streets, then look further. Finally, you may plan for greater expectations of children in their use of geographical skills: initial studies of the local climate, for example, require them to stick symbols for types of weather on a big chart; later, they use simple instruments to take readings of the weather; then they could use a computer spreadsheet to analyse weather patterns over time.

Localities are not isolated bubbles in the landscape. They are connected to the world in many ways. Any enquiry into a locality needs to include how that locality is affected by events elsewhere, as well as how the locality has an influence on other places. For example, when investigating an **urban area** with a **port**, we could examine where ships were coming from and what they brought into the country. We could then investigate the cargoes exported from there and where they went to. The River Tees **harbour** authority provides local schools with excellent data about this. It enables children to learn how places and people around the world are interconnected and depend on each other.

As teachers, we have to create and provide many and varied learning resources. Literacy texts and maths apparatus are essential teaching tools. Geography is interesting in that while we do have to provide many geographical resources, a study of the children's locality enables them to provide much existing knowledge and understanding themselves. By working this way, we can build on the real interests of children. They come to school with experiences of their physical world, such as knowing where the best slopes for skating are. They already have some understanding of human geography, for example the post office sells better sweets than the local shop, but they have to travel further to get them; they have a favourite place where they play with their friends; adults at home may have told them exactly how far away they may play and no further because of perceived dangers. Good geography planning can build on these local experiences.

Localities further afield can also be investigated. By choosing a highly contrasting locality in another part of the United Kingdom, you can introduce children to the similarities and differences that exist within any country. By choosing a locality to study in another country, children can begin to understand how people live in other places and investigate events in the physical world that do not happen in their locality. For example, *Why do some people still decide to* **farm** *in places where they could easily be affected by earthquakes?*

Why you need to know these facts

Locality studies are key building blocks of a good geography curriculum. Teachers do need to be clear about the opportunities each type of locality study can create. You need to feel confident that you know what the localities contain and how you can use them. There are seven years of primary education for children to cover the required localities. This means that schools need to plan the sequence of locality studies their children will experience.

This should be tied in with fieldwork plans. The skills, knowledge and understanding to be learned need to be carefully mapped onto these plans. The facts in this section give a clear idea of how locality enquiries can form the basis of your geography lessons.

Vocabulary

Place – there is no one definition of a place. It can cover a small or large area. It can have any shape and be located anywhere in the world. It's a flexible concept and that is one of its strengths. A place can be a corner of the school field that we wish to investigate; it can be somewhere distant that has suffered an earthquake.

Locality – for the purposes of this book, this is defined as an area around your school in which you study geography. It is also the area you define in another part of Britain or the world that you choose as another locality to study. This might be a village in Mexico or a suburb of Nantes where your European link school is located.

Common misconceptions

A locality is a whole country.
This misconception occurs in both teachers' and pupils' planning, especially when looking at localities in other countries. Also, if you teach in a village school and want to study a contrasting town, don't use the whole town – take a part of it that is about the same size as your agreed school locality. Look for a part of the town that has features you want to investigate. Keep all the localities in your geography programme about the same size to help children to study the comparisons.

The content of your locality study does not stand still. Well thought out whole-school planning will enable you to adapt the content as the world changes. This makes the geography more relevant to the children and more interesting for you to teach. That's perhaps where geography is different from some other subjects: the processes remain similar but the content should reflect a constantly changing world.

A country or region in Europe can be studied as a locality and there are ample areas to select, all of which have individual aspects which will be of interest. For example, Poland, which until recently may have been considered a less economically developed country, is counted as a more economically developed country since its accession to the EU and all of the investment that has entailed. Furthermore, it has a rich culture, history and values, all of which could help children to build positive attitudes towards other people around the world and perhaps begin to question the nature of 'development'. A locality like Poland would also enable a theme such as the changing uses of land to be examined. Many schools in the UK may well have pupils of Polish origin or ancestry so the cultural links between Poland and the UK could also be examined.

Handy tip

● Train yourself to 'think locality study'! Always be on the lookout for suitable resources. A local newspaper article about an environmental issue might be the starting point of an effective enquiry.
● Be aware of resources that should be kept for use in the future. A set of local photographs taken today, for example, could be an excellent history resource for your successors in five or ten years' time.

Teaching ideas

A local study

Questions and issues make very good starting points for a local study:
● What do we want in our new school garden? Where should the flowers and bushes be placed so they grow well?
● What is the best route to take around our locality to deliver the fliers advertising our summer fair?
● What are the advantages and disadvantages of the new supermarket being built on derelict land near our school?
● How do people use rivers around the world? What effects does this have and how do rivers affect people?

● Would a virtual school bus help to solve some of the traffic and pollution problems in our locality?

Careful planning can resolve some of the problems of time constraints in covering everything described above. Think carefully about building geographical themes into locality work. Be very clear about the geographical skills, knowledge and understanding that you intend to develop. Plan for children to use ICT to enhance their understanding.

Keep the idea of scale in your mind at all times. Help children to make links between their locality, events and places at a national scale and the wider world. For example, while studying your local river, compare it with another river in the United Kingdom and perhaps use a news item about an environmental issue or natural disaster occurring on a river in another country.

Your school and the locality

Subject facts

When you are choosing features to investigate, be very clear about the geographical skills, knowledge and understanding you wish to develop. For example, investigate where to place a new flowerbed if you want children to investigate why features are located in certain places in the world. Then, carefully select those aspects that will help you do this to the best advantage. If you are looking at changes, children can study the different types of transport using a local road at different times of day.

Inside the school

A lot of good geography can be done inside the school building. The following questions are designed to start you thinking about how you might use your school. Each school is unique so the answers will depend on your school.

● What are the different parts used for? This introduces the idea of land use.

● What journeys do people make around school?

● Do various parts of the school have a different feel to them? Are some warm and cosy while others are gloomy?

- What building materials have been used?
- What textures, shapes and patterns can be found in the building?

The school contains a lot of mathematical information. Think about, for example, how many doors there are in the school. You and the children may be surprised at the answer! Marking them on a simple plan introduces the concepts of key, symbol and location.

Can you work out why the school was designed as it was? Geographically, this helps you to explain why things are where they are.

The school grounds

The school grounds are an excellent starting point for a local study at KS1. They provide an easily accessible, safe and cheap resource, but familiarity can sometimes hide the opportunities present. All school grounds are unique, but the following considerations will guide you into seeing the geographical opportunities they offer:

- They provide a space to play directional games that help to teach geographical language: *left, right, north, west, up, down, around, beside* and so on.
- Children can look for patterns, shapes and textures; rubbings can be made and their positions marked on simple plans.
- Simple weather observations can be made in the grounds.
- Different parts can be compared. For instance, which are the windiest places? Why is this?
- The grounds will throw up environmental issues, such as why is there a lot of litter in a particular place? Where is the best place to put a new litter bin?
- What do children think and feel about different parts of the grounds? Are some bright and happy and others exciting?
- What is available to use for surveying and collecting data? What is the temperature in different places? Why does it vary?
- What opportunities are there for children to really observe carefully? Get them to look ahead, up and down, and through various views. All this helps to put that place into a broader context for young children.
- Use all your senses. What can be seen, heard and smelled coming from beyond the grounds without actually leaving them? What is making that cooking smell we sometimes get in the playground? It may be a nearby bakery.

The school locality

When you and your colleagues have defined a realistic limit for your school locality, make time to find out what it contains for geographical study. As you find features, think about the skills, knowledge and understanding they will help children to learn.

● What buildings are in the locality? Do they occur in patterns, for example parallel streets of houses?
● What are they used for? What do people do there?
● What types of land use can you find?
● What shopping facilities are there?
● What evidence is there for this place being linked to others? For example, a study of the local bus timetable can explain why people need to make certain journeys.
● What do different parts of the locality feel like to be in?
● What environmental issues exist? Are there a lot of empty houses? Why is this?
● How might local people help children with their enquiries? A local road haulage company might show children which European countries their drivers travel to and what they carry.
● What mapping, sketching and surveying opportunities exist?
● What landscape features are present, for example slopes, streams, erosion?
● What transport and communication is present?
● What leisure facilities are there?
● What services can be studied, for example a local fire station?
● What secondary sources can you find? Local people and facilities, such as branch libraries and tourist information centres, can be good starting points.

Chapter 6 provides factual ideas for developing these questions in the locality.

Why you need to know these facts

The school and its locality provide an easily accessible and relatively cheap geographical resource for learning. At KS1, children should study the locality of their school in order to learn the relevant geography skills, knowledge and understanding required at that age level.

Vicinity – the area immediately surrounding the school.

Common misconceptions

A *locality* is a large area.
This is not necessarily true. If your school is in a town, it is not the whole town. At KS1, it is the immediate vicinity of the school. At KS2, it will cover the area in which the children's homes are located. Both of these provide an easily accessible area to study and use to build on children's experiences.

Teaching ideas

Essential resources
Ask people in school for maps, plans and photographs that may be around. These are essential resources to use and adapt. For example, some photographs taken five years ago will help young children see how a place they know has changed. The caretaker may have the architect's plans from which you can make a simple outline plan of the school.

Creating resources
Finally, with a little imagination, the school grounds can help to create other geographical resources. Get your pupils to choose a view of the grounds and arrange to take a photograph of it each week for a year. The resulting set of prints will be an excellent resource for work with young children on seasons, patterns, change and sequencing.

Choosing another locality

Subject facts

When you have considered the questions in the section above (pages 46–48), you should have a great deal of factual information and ideas about your locality. The next stage is to decide what you want your other UK locality to contain. If you are planning comparative studies, both places may need some similar features. For example, if you plan to cover changing land use, you will need clear examples, perhaps where farm land has recently been built on in each place, but with different new types of use.

Your local area will contain some of the features that you want to look at, but not others. For example, you may be a long way from the coast. If your plans include the study of coasts to develop geographical concepts, a coastal locality can be chosen. This will help to develop enquiries into physical and human differences.

You need to have access to relevant and up-to-date resources about your contrasting locality. A very effective way of doing this is to find a school there that would like to exchange resources with you. In this way, children have a real reason for doing research and presenting their findings. Many types of resource can be made and exchanged, helping to integrate ICT firmly into the school geography curriculum:

● maps and plans – new and historical, at a variety of scales
● photographs – ground level and aerial
● videos
● emails and faxes
● artefacts, such as local stone, newspapers and recipes, and things made locally, such as pottery
● data, for example weather records, exchanged electronically
● snippets from local television and radio
● toys and games
● children's fiction from their country
● songs and dances.

Finally, there are commercial packs available on localities around the UK. Many are very good, but they cannot contain the wealth of information and perspectives that you might obtain from school exchanges and fieldwork.

A locality in a less economically developed country

This locality could be selected from a country within Africa, Asia or South and Central America, including the Caribbean. The choice of location in this case is usually governed by the resources available (see 'Resources' at the end of this chapter). However, other factors to consider when choosing a foreign locality to study include:

● availability of published materials like locality packs
● personal or school contacts through parents, local industry and so on
● support from agencies such as ActionAid **www.actionaid.org.uk** who can supply contacts or visitors to school
● ICT links – suitable websites, email and webcam links to schools and sites of interest, television series.

Why you need to know these facts

Studying a contrasting locality gives children a chance to investigate similarities and differences with their school locality. If you keep these facts in mind, you will be able to focus clearly on exactly what you want children to learn.

Vocabulary

Economically developed – this focuses on the wealth of a country or place. It's important to balance this when working with children to ensure they also understand that such a country may have highly developed arts, music and **agricultural** skills that may be more sustainable than in so-called more developed countries.

Common misconceptions

Contrasting localities do not need to be a long way from your school. For example, if your school is in a suburb of Leeds, a village locality in the Yorkshire Dales could make an appropriate contrasting UK locality. It could also mean that inexpensive and time-effective fieldwork can take place.

Another locality can also contain features found in the school locality. This will help you to develop the teaching of geographical themes. For example, your local river can be compared to a river found in the other locality.

Handy tip

Keep in touch with teachers who work in other places. They may well be looking for a locality just like yours, and theirs may be ideal for you.

Teaching ideas

Questions and answers

Links with a school in your contrasting locality are good reasons for asking questions and finding answers. Each class could write a few questions about everyday life, such as:

- Where are the newest buildings and what are they for?
- What are your favourite places and why?
- Where does your family buy most of their food?

Join the lists so that both groups of children answer all the questions. This will root the enquiries firmly within children's experience and introduce them to finding reasons for similarities and differences around the world.

Rural places

Subject facts

Land not covered in urban areas is called *rural*. Rural land is used in many different ways:

- Some is wild, open country, owned by someone or an organisation, but not actually used for anything. Parts of central Wales are like this.

● Some is wild, open country used for **agriculture** that fits the climate and soils. Sheep farming in the Yorkshire **Moors** is an example.

● Woodland may be wild wood or managed and sustained forests used for timber production. Hamsterley Forest in County Durham is an example of the latter.

● Farm land accounts for much of the rural land in the UK. The farming that takes places on it will depend on location, soils, climate, local traditions and demands, as well as current economic and political pressures. For example, high prices for oilseed rape products mean more is being grown on farms.

● Industrial land use can be found in rural areas. Stone **quarries**, open-cast coal mines and factory sites are examples of these.

● Rural settlements take much of the remaining land.

Dispersed settlement patterns can be seen where cottages, farms and hamlets are scattered across a landscape. These occur when the land can only support a few people.

Sometimes settlements are nucleated because buildings have grown up close together. These create villages of different shapes and sizes. Figure 4 shows some village shapes that children will find on maps and on field visits.

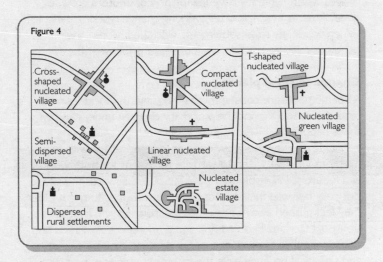

Figure 4

Cross-shaped nucleated village

Compact nucleated village

T-shaped nucleated village

Semi-dispersed village

Linear nucleated village

Nucleated green village

Dispersed rural settlements

Nucleated estate village

● Cross-shaped nucleated villages grew up where two roads met, often as a trading point for people using each road.

● Compact nucleated villages developed where a number of roads met.

- T-shaped nucleated villages occur where one road meets and ends at a second. Again, this was a place where people from various places could meet.
- Semi-dispersed villages exist where the land can only support a few people.
- Linear villages can be found in the Fens in Eastern England, growing up along the straight roads that were set out following the draining of the landscape.
- Nucleated **green villages** often grew up around an area of common land. Animals were kept here for protection.
- Housing for groups of workers developed during the industrial revolution around new industrial sites. The Durham coal-pit villages are an example of this.

Geographers in the past often concentrated on how the physical landscape influenced the location, shape and size of a settlement. This is clearly important, but today we also look closely at economic, social and technological reasons. For instance, a picturesque village just outside a busy city will grow as it attracts people who can afford to pay the house prices and have the transport to commute to work. In the future, will villages which currently have few or no **commuters** grow as developments in ICT and teleworking change working patterns? When you study rural settlements with the children, their enquiries need to consider various reasons for what they find.

Change in rural places

All settlements are constantly changing, and this includes rural settlements too. We can help primary children understand why this is happening if we use the idea of 'push-pull factors'.

Young people who grow up in an isolated village with few functions can feel pulled towards larger places for both work and leisure. Old people may have felt pulled towards the village originally because their friends were there, but as they get older they feel pushed away because of the isolation and limited transport facilities. People living and working in busy towns and cities feel pulled towards the village because it offers a quiet and safe location. They have the income to provide their own transport, so distance from other places and lack of services doesn't worry them. The cumulative effect of all these push-pull factors helps to create the current structure and functions of a rural settlement.

The term *rural mosaic* is used to help explain the structure of rural settlements. With few people working in agriculture today it is too simplistic to see rural places as centred on countryside functions alone. They contain people with a wide range of jobs, lifestyles, aspirations, hopes and values. Village functions can have different meanings to people in various parts of the mosaic: the village store may be the main source of goods for a retired resident with limited money to use on transport; for the commuter it is an added convenience to use if they forget something at the out-of-town **hypermarket**. As children find out what is happening in rural places, they can build up a picture of the rural mosaic that explains what they find.

The mosaic can vary depending on where the rural settlement is located. Geographers identify the *rural-urban fringe* as the area where towns and cities are growing out into the countryside. Villages here can have rising land values, fewer services as those in the town creep closer to them, and changes in the make-up of the residents. The picture could be quite different in a village of similar size many miles from a town or city.

Rural deprivation is another way in which geographers view the countryside. They pick out a number of features, interesting due to their similarity with inner-city deprivation:

- unemployment
- low wages
- decline in services
- population decline
- inaccessibility
- reduced morale
- little new investment
- skills not in demand
- high cost of public services.

Why you need to know these facts

Rural places are constantly changing. It's not always easy to understand what is happening, especially if the locality under investigation is your own – familiarity is not always helpful. The ideas above provide ways of looking objectively at rural places. They may also be helpful when studying distant rural places. Your chosen developing-country locality may depend heavily on farming, but changes might be beginning to happen. For instance, international retailers may be encouraging production of certain high-value vegetables for export, and this will start to change the locality.

Common misconceptions

Rural places are just part of the countryside in the United Kingdom.

This is not necessarily the case. They are complex and interconnected. We cannot explain them simply as agricultural and isolated. Some are, but most have complex links with other places.

Teaching ideas

Researching change

Research your rural locality to find a geographical question that will help children to understand what happens there and how it is changing due to links with other places. Why is there only one village shop, whereas a map from the 1960s shows four shops in the village? Why are there more houses in our village built after 1970 than older ones?

Local resources can be an excellent starting point. Photographs on old village postcards, bus timetables, old and new maps and plans at various scales, and from local people and newspaper articles can all provide clues about how your rural locality is changing.

Urban places

Subject facts

There is no one universally accepted definition of the word *urban*. However, geographers use a number of indicators to help to identify the process of **urbanisation**. Urban places can be identified as having:

- a large population size, often with a high density
- specific urban features, such as a **central business district** and different **residential zones**
- specific economic functions, such as services and manufacturing
- administrative activity.

Some people suggest that a country is becoming more urbanised when the number of people living in towns and cities is growing faster than the population as a whole.

Urbanisation

Urbanisation is a process that is constantly changing. It is interesting to examine the stages of urbanisation as they can also be used when studying less economically developed countries.

Urbanisation often begins slowly, with most people living in rural areas and working in rural activities. It then becomes much more rapid as more and more people are drawn toward the perceived benefits of living in the city. This is currently happening in many less economically developed countries. Mexico City had a population of 2.9 million in 1950. This had grown to 18 million by 1995 and by 2012 was 20.5 million.

Counter-urbanisation then starts to occur. Features of urbanisation such as congestion, pollution and overall quality of life encourage those who can to move out of the city and commute to work. Businesses often relocate from the centre to the suburbs.

Finally, *re-urbanisation* can take place as city centres and suburbs are renewed and sometimes **gentrified**.

All these processes affect the surrounding areas:

- Urban sprawl occurs.
- Local agriculture and natural **habitats** are affected: the demand for fresh fruit and vegetables may change what farms around cities decide to grow.
- Transport demands increase and become congested.
- The quality of social and personal life changes – larger towns can generate more traffic noise or make some people feel more lonely.

To help children understand a built-up area, it is important to study:

- the location and site
- the pattern of settlements in the landscape
- the shape or form of the area

- the function of the settlement and its position in a hierachy of places
- how it is changing.

Children can study towns and cities to identify and explain patterns and processes taking place within them. Although every city is unique, there are many interesting similarities between them. For example, they all have a centre and the oldest parts of the city are normally there. As you give children the chance to study various cities, they will begin to see the similarities and differences. In general it is possible to identify particular areas of cities and large towns. Starting at the centre they are:

1. *Capital or primate city.* This is a town or city containing government departments and the seat of government.

2. *Central business district (CBD).* A central area can be identified in nearly all towns and cities. It is called the central business district and is often one of the oldest parts. Central locations are supposed to be the most accessible, but the huge increase in traffic means that this advantage is decreasing. A number of interesting things happen in the CBD:

- Land values are high, so buildings often have many stories. Vertical zoning occurs in these stories, with floors being used for different functions.
- Offices and administrative functions develop. Head offices and government departments can often be found.
- The central location attracts high-quality and specialised **retailing**.
- Many types of transport converge there, such as railway stations and bus depots.
- The population is normally low. However those who do live there are often wealthy dwellers in luxury flats, while there are homeless people living on the streets or in hostels.
- The land in the CBD is used for different purposes that are often grouped together, such as when estate agents' offices are found on one or two streets of a town.
- The CBD does not stay in the same place forever. Sometimes this change occurs naturally, but it can be planned, as in the London Docklands development.

3. *Inner-city areas.* These normally surround the CBD. Geographers identify a number of features in these areas:

- Housing is old and badly maintained.
- Few jobs in the declining manufacturing industries result in high unemployment.

- Crime levels tend to be higher than elsewhere.
- Facilities are limited and of poor quality.
- Large numbers of **immigrants** can lead to racial tension.
- The population is ageing as it is not mobile.
- Environmental quality is poor.

However, as with many geographical ideas, this is at one end of a continuum. Many inner-city areas have vibrant communities with organisations such as schools working extremely hard to improve lives and aspirations. It is vital to avoid stereotypical definitions of any place, but to see its current situation as part of an ongoing process. The positive changes can be remarkable. However, as demand for living space increases, some of these deprived areas are identified by developers who invest heavily and gentrify the locality. This brings in new services, such as restaurants, but forces any remaining poor inhabitants into other areas. Northern Manchester is an example of this process: it was fashionable in the late 19th and early 20th centuries but declined rapidly after 1945. Today it is thriving again.
4. *Suburbs.* These surround the central part of cities. As people need more places to live and work, suburbs have extended out into the countryside around cities. They often grow up along the roads and railways leading away from cities. Sometimes they develop around villages near the city.

Urban deprivation

Urban deprivation has been identified as a growing and widespread problem in Britain. It occurs in most towns and cities, even apparently wealthy ones like Oxford and Bath. It exists in areas containing poor-quality housing and concentrations of homeless people. There are many complex reasons for this growth, but unemployment is accepted as central. A current concern is the identification of suburban decline that is similar to the problems identified in inner-city areas.

The function of the settlement

Geographers identify a range of features and processes in towns and cities for study. Children can investigate these in their enquiries to better understand what a place is like:
- *Land use and changes in it.* How is land use changing? Why is it changing?
- *Population size and structure.* How many people live there? Are there more retired people in the area? Why?

- *Transport routes and facilities.* Which are the main roads and what are they used for? Are there any dangerous roads or junctions? Why?
- *Environmental quality.* In which direction is pollution from local factories blown by the wind? How might people be encouraged to travel to work and shops using bicycles?
- *Employment opportunities.* What jobs do people have? Why are new jobs in ICT services growing in the locality?
- *Services provided.* What shops are found in the town centre? Do people have to travel to another place to visit a hospital? Why?
- *Links with other places.* Which parts of the world have new arrivals come from and why? Where have the **raw materials** for local industry come from and where do the finished products go?
- *The effects of ICT and global changes.* Has internet shopping cut down traffic problems in the town centre? Which countries grow the fruit and vegetables found in the local supermarket?

These features can be studied in relation to towns and cities of all sizes. However, there are some towns and cities that have grown in a particular way or for a particular reason. One group is those that have one main specialist function. Seaside **resorts** such as Torquay and commuter towns like Crawley are examples. A commuter town is one where people live but travel out of for their work. Seaside resorts gain most of their income from money brought in by holidaymakers. In Britain, we also have 32 new towns and cities that have been built since 1945. Early new towns such as Welwyn **Garden City** and Stevenage are very different from the more recently established ones like Milton Keynes. Each one was carefully designed and based on the changing ideas of planners, sociologists, economists, industrialists and politicians. More recently, a range of modern developments, such as Cambourne in Cambridgeshire, have been built and the government has even proposed the development of a group of **eco towns**.

Why you need to know these facts

 Towns and cities contain a great variety of features and processes, gradually changing with time. If you select a locality within a town or city, it will represent just a part of the whole picture.

It is important for both you and your pupils to learn how and why it is as you find it. Settlements are an important theme in geography and offer exciting and interesting environments in which children can work.

Vocabulary

Central business district – the busy centre of a town or city.
Counter-urbanisation – a process seen in towns and cities in highly advanced countries such as the USA, New Zealand, Sweden and Britain. It describes the net loss of population from towns and cities. Urban dwellers who can afford to move into the country create this process. Some then commute back to towns to work, some work from rural homes using developments in ICT and many are retired.
Eco town – name given to a housing scheme which has an emphasis on affordable and sustainable living.
New town – a town deliberately planned for a purpose. Town planning goes back a long way. For example, James Craig designed the New Town area in Edinburgh in the 18th century. The majority of new towns in England were built following the New Town Act of 1947. Early examples are Stevenage and Crawley. Milton Keynes is still growing.
Suburbs – the areas around the centres of towns and cities.
Urban deprivation – areas of towns and cities with few facilities and a poor-quality environment.
Urbanisation – the spread of towns and cities as they become bigger and take up land previously used for agriculture, and other open spaces.
Urban sprawl – the growth of built-up areas with little direct planning and design.

Common misconceptions

● An urban locality in the context of primary geography is not a whole town or city. Keep its size to an area that can easily be walked to from school.

● A contrasting locality in the UK does not need to be a long way from the school: all the children need to be able to do is study other ways of life and natural features.

Handy tip

Try to define an urban locality that has a range of functions, such as various types of living places, job opportunities and land use. This will provide wider opportunities for children to develop their knowledge, understanding and skills.

Teaching ideas

Using playmats
Geography suppliers now offer playmats printed with an aerial photograph centred on your school. KS1 children enjoy using these to: find their homes; mark their journeys to school with wool; identify roads, houses and trees and spot their favourite play spaces. They can ask about features that they can't identify, and other children may be able to provide the answers.

Using maps
Find an old map of the part of your town or village that you plan to study that includes your school site. An old school may be shown, but a new school will not. Choose a map with a scale of 1:1250 so children can see plenty of detail. Get children to list what they find on the map. They could then work in carefully supervised groups in the locality to see what features are still there and what has changed. This will lead them into researching why the changes happened.

Using photographs
Visit the local studies centre in your town or city library. Choose and arrange to have copied a range of old photographs of your locality. Take photographs of the same places today and get children to match each pair of photographs. Then ask them to describe and list the changes they see. Arrange to visit some of the places in the photographs and get children to plot clues seen on the old photographs onto large-scale maps of the locality.

Using computers

Scan a photograph of part of your locality into a paint package. After discussing the changes seen in the old photographs activity on the previous page, ask children to adapt the scanned image to show what they think the area might look like when they are 50 years old. Ask them to word-process their reasons for the changes they show. These documents can then be displayed alongside current and historical photographs of your locality.

Localities in less economically developed countries

Subject facts

Geographers study the development of countries by looking at four main features:
- the rate and level of economic progress
- the impact and use of technology
- levels and distribution of social, cultural and political freedom
- justice and human rights.

A range of features is used to assess the level of development of a country:
- life expectancy
- **infant mortality**
- literacy levels
- levels of urbanisation
- manufacturing workforce
- income per head.

These are often used together to build up a broader picture.

The World Bank has classified countries into these types:
- industrial market economies, such as Japan and the UK
- centrally planned economies, for example Cuba
- high-income oil exporters, for example Saudi Arabia
- middle-income developing countries, like Brazil
- low-income developing countries, such as Malawi.

Many indicators are available to assess the level of development and each one has advantages and disadvantages. Gross National Product (GNP) per head is widely used.

Our perceptions of development

Much of our knowlege about the developing world is supplied by fundraising agencies and the media. This has created a distorted understanding and public perception. The media highlights extreme problems, while fundraising organisations want to increase income. Some geographers prefer to provide an alternative view of our current world.

Education

Many organisations suggest that education is the key to raising levels of development. Higher levels of education amongst girls has been shown to reduce population growth and infant mortality, and improve children's health.

Poverty and health

Infant mortality rates (IMRs) are often used to assess levels of development. They refer to the number of children per 1000 who die before their first birthday. In 2012, IMRs for the UK stood at 5.01 (that is 5.01 deaths per 1000 infants). The lowest IMRs were for Singapore (2.30) with the highest in Angola (a staggering 184.44 deaths per 1000). More children die from malnutrition than any other cause. Many who survive are physically and mentally affected for the rest of their lives.

The effect of aid on development

Countries receive aid in three ways:
- Multilateral aid given by a number of countries. Sums are not huge and interest rates on the loans can be high.
- Bilateral aid from one country, often with rules attached to benefit the provider.
- Non-government organisations (NGOs), for example Save the Children. They often have specialist knowledge and skills to make long-term effective use of aid. They are less restricted by government rules and can react flexibly.

Geographers identify a number of ways in which aid is provided for development:
- Top-down development. Large-scale projects controlled by governments, including emergency relief projects.
- Bottom-up development. This is small-scale work created alongside communities in an attempt to find long-term solutions that will improve living standards.

● Appropriate development. This makes use of resources such as local skills and technology that geographers understand to develop standards of living. It is based on the values and culture of the region.
● Sustainable development. These projects aim to improve standards of living while safeguarding natural resources for future generations.

Why you need to know these facts

The concept of development can be complex. The reasons why a country is less economically developed than others may be hard to identify. It can easily become a very negative way of looking at a locality and the people within it, so it is important to be aware of the richness of the culture, heritage, values and skills.

Common misconceptions

Many children think that all people in economically developing regions have similar problems. Media images of starving people riddled with disease and unable to help themselves are common. This attitude is often reinforced by other factors in children's lives, such as family members.

Teaching ideas

Developing understanding
Perhaps part of your main role in helping children to understand a developing country is to enable them to:
● Assess a range of evidence in trying to understand what is actually happening there.
● Understand that events in one country may be highly affected by events elsewhere.
● Understand that people in severe need also have values and ideas to be respected, and the way we support their development should take this into account.
● Be aware of stereotypes that have been created.

Finally, there may be opportunities to consider what development and sustainable development mean for us. How far along the development route might some cultures wish to go? Is our own so-called 'developed' consumer lifestyle actually sustainable or necessary? It is also important to make connections with localities much nearer to home. There is a growing number of people in the United Kingdom who have severe health and education needs, are homeless or poorly fed. Development is certainly not just a global concept. It is often right beside us in our own localities.

The European dimension

Subject facts

At KS1, children should be provided with the opportunity to study a locality overseas that has physical and/or human features that contrast with those in the locality of the school. At KS2, in their study of localities and themes children should study a range of places and environments in different parts of the world, including the United Kingdom and the European Union.

A locality of similar size to your school's can be selected from other European countries. When children study distant places, such as a village in Mexico, it can be relatively easy for them to focus on the differences in ways of life. Studying people and places in European countries makes children look in more detail at similarities and differences, as they can be harder to pinpoint.

Many children visit other European countries as tourists on holiday. This can provide a very restricted view of people and places. Studying a European locality can help to balance the tourist images of some countries.

Being physically close to mainland Europe it is possible to build a European residential visit into the whole-school visits policy. This would enable children to gain first-hand experience of another place, people and culture. They can apply enquiry skills learned earlier and study some of the themes, such as settlements or rivers.

Including a European dimension also helps children learn about geographical change. Comparing maps of Europe drawn over the last 100 years shows how countries change name, borders and resources. It enables many current aspects of the news to be integrated into the curriculum, for example why do some people want to come to live in the UK?

There are many links between countries around Europe that help children to understand key geographical ideas:

- Huge quantities of food travel between European countries – why?
- Environmental problems ignore national boundaries – pollution from British power stations affects forests in Scandinavia.
- Children can see many European products available in Britain – why do we buy goods from Ikea and BMW?

Although modern foreign languages are not statutory in primary schools, studying a European locality is an excellent way of introducing children to another language. What are the Spanish words for *town, farm, road* and *beach*? How can we ask simple questions in German? Schools already linked with other European schools often remark that children are highly motivated to use another language to talk to the children and teachers. Schools in other countries also value such links, as their curriculum often includes learning English, which can be developed through the exchange of geographical and other ideas.

Why you need to know these facts

Many schools often focus their geography case studies on locations in the UK, and they do not make full use of the opportunity provided by the wealth of interesting European locations available to study. A good school curriculum will seize this opportunity by examining a range of European countries, and comparing and contrasting them with the UK. This is of particular importance as Europe and the European Union are increasingly relevant to us in terms of business, travel and culture.

Common misconceptions

There is no time to develop a European dimension in an already overloaded primary curriculum.

There are two ways to overcome this:

The first is to develop units of study with a clear European focus. This could be a locality in another European country. It might also be linked to a theme in which comparisons are made between places. For instance, a school near the River Severn could study both this river and the River Rhine or another European river. Interesting similarities and differences would be found, both in terms of the physical features of the rivers and the uses people make of them.

The second is to make use of opportunities for a European focus across other subject areas. You could, for example: study European landscapes to provide ideas for art and design; encourage children to listen to music from around Europe.

Questions

Which countries are part of Europe?

There is no one answer to this question, but teachers often spend too long worrying about a possible answer. It entirely depends on why you are asking the question. Many countries are linked through various treaties and agreements: some are economic while others are for agricultural or environmental issues. Membership is constantly changing, so definitive and time-proof lists are impossible to provide.

Handy tip

One of the most effective ways to study a European locality or theme is to link with a school in one or more other countries. The Central Bureau for Educational Visits and Exchanges, 10 Spring Gardens, London, SW1A 2BN (020 7389 4004) should be able to provide all the information you need to get started. The British Council has excellent provision to help schools make links with other European schools. See the following websites (the second one is for setting up international school links):
www.schoolsintoeurope.com
schoolsonline.britishcouncil.org

Teaching ideas

Links with a European school

When you have made links with a European school, an effective way to begin studying each other's localities is to exchange a set of numbered colour photographs and a large-scale map of your locality. Keep a set in school for reference. There are many benefits to this. The first is that your children will have to decide what to show on their photographs. This will require that they know the locality and begin to think about how selective photographs of places can be. When they receive questions from the other school, they will have a reason to research as well as a ready-made audience for their local enquiries.

ICT can easily be integrated into this planning through the use of digital cameras to take photographs, emails to transmit information and desktop publishing for editing text and graphics.

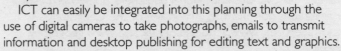

Resources

Useful reading: Geographical enquiry

Achieving QTS. Teaching Primary Geography by Catling, S. & Willy, T. (Exeter: Learning Matters, 2009).

Geography 3–11. A guide for Teachers by Cooper, H., Rowley, C. & Asquith, S. (London: Fulton, 2006).

Teaching Geography in Primary Schools by Martin, F. (Cambridge: Chris Kington Publishing, 2006).

'Focus on connecting with landscapes', *Primary Geographer*, Number 70 (Sheffield: Geographical Association, Autumn 2009).

Websites

www.geograph.org.uk

www.earthcam.com

www.geography.org/uk/cpdevents/onlinecpd

www.earthobservatory.nasa.gov

www.globaldimension.org.uk

Physical resources

Towns and cities offer a very wide range of sources of information that you can use in your enquiries: the locality itself – buildings, transport types, people, environmental issues; libraries and information centres; council offices and archives; urban studies centres; urban development corporation offices; websites; newspaper, television and radio offices; museums and galleries; cyber cafés; historical and heritage sites; private organisations, for example estate agents; public services, such as the police; environmental agencies and action groups.

Foreign countries

It can be hard to get up-to-date information about distant places, so you may decide to choose one of the many packs available from various educational publishers, non-government organisations (for example, ActionAid) or the Geographical Association. See: **www.actionaid.org.uk** and **www.geography. org.uk**

The best provide detailed teacher's notes and information. They normally contain A4 colour photographs, maps, plans and geographical data. Many include photocopiable sheets for children to use. You could add to these with information from the following sources: the national embassy in London; the internet; geography textbooks, atlases and globes; CD-ROMs and computer software; television and radio programmes; visitors; tourist information; artefacts, including toys; emails.

Patterns and processes

Geographers are interested in finding patterns and processes in our world. They record them, interpret them and suggest explanations for what they see happening. As they find out more, these explanations change. Patterns and processes can be seen in the physical and natural world and in human activity on Earth.

This chapter begins by identifying the difference between patterns and processes as geographers see them. It then looks at eight aspects of geography that can easily come into your teaching and gives an explanation of the patterns and processes within each one. These aspects are weather and climate, ecosystems, population, settlements, land use, tectonic patterns and processes, weathering, and soils. The last three of these sections look at geographical patterns and processes in the physical world and their relationship with human activity.

Patterns

Subject facts

Geographers use the word *pattern* to describe the way in which physical and human features occur or are arranged.

Physical feature: rivers

All over the world, there are many different rivers. Some are huge, such as the Amazon, while others, such as the River Swale in Yorkshire, are relatively small. But if we looked at a map showing the courses of both of these rivers, we would see many patterns and similarities: they both have many tributaries that feed water into them; they begin high up in hilly or mountainous places; the water in both flows downhill and eventually reaches the sea.

> ### A bird's eye view
> Find a satellite image of a whole country – almost any will do. If you half-close your eyes and look at the more hilly or mountainous places, you will begin to see the patterns made as streams and rivers have cut their way through the landscape. It takes time for these to come into focus, but keep looking – it's part of becoming a geographer! Many of these patterns have shapes similar to that of a tree in winter: the smaller twigs and branches representing the patterns of streams and the trunk of the tree representing the main part of the river.

Physical feature: landscape

Patterns can be seen in the countryside too. Devon has a unique sense of place when you walk there: the granite rock has eroded to produce particular shapes and patterns across the landscape; the warm climate creates conditions for particular species to grow; the bedrock has eroded to produce a rich soil for farming.

Human feature: towns

People have placed many patterns on the Earth. Find a street map of your nearest town. Don't just look at individual streets and roads, but start to look for patterns. You are very likely to see rows of straight and quite tightly packed streets very close to the town centre. These were probably built in the 19th century and may have names such as Victoria Terrace and Gladstone Street. Many of those street patterns would probably have another pattern built into them – that of a distribution of corner shops. How many of them are still there today? What are they used for? How might you answer these questions? Again, the answers show how society is changing and adapting. A geographer would expect to see some evidence of a British town growing in this way.

Extending the scale, a geographer would not predict this if looking at a street map of a Spanish town, where Spain's history and culture have led to a different range of reasons to explain the street patterns. On the other hand, a geographer *would* expect to find evidence on both Spanish and British street plans that many roads led to the town centre and that a number of features could be found there, for example banks and municipal offices.

Street patterns tell us a lot about a town. Have a look at the edges of your map or town plan to see the more recent building patterns. You'll probably see estates where all the roads are quite short and curved, many of them being cul-de-sacs. During the past 35 years or so, planners and developers have used this layout of streets for a number of reasons. It can reduce traffic flow and make the streets safer, and the social engineers say it helps to develop a sense of community by breaking down large estates into more identifiable neighbourhoods and communities.

Human feature: countryside
Patterns can be seen in the countryside too. Roads follow narrow, deep valleys and sometimes cut across high moorlands. Many villages nestle in sheltered valleys. Estuaries provide locations for fishing villages, and tourism is often attracted to such areas by a mild climate and attractive scenery.

Why you need to know these facts

Children in KS1 and KS2 are required to develop a knowledge and understanding of geographical patterns. It is important that you understand the geographical meaning of the pattern.

Vocabulary

Pattern – the way in which physical and human features occur or are arranged on the Earth.
Physical features – aspects of the world that occur naturally, for example a stream.
Human features – parts of the world created or adapted by people, for example a **canal**.

Common misconceptions

Children are not able to recognise and understand patterns at an early age.

They can begin to see and understand patterns in the world if we provide them with simple experiences. For example, the class hamster always seems to sleep in the same place in its cage; puddles form in the same parts of the playground each time it rains; different age groups of children in the school tend to play in their own areas.

Handy tip

Keep the examples of the patterns your pupils investigate simple. Why do they think the hamster likes to sleep in that particular place? Is it because it's near the radiator and so warm? Do puddles form because that part of the playground is shaped like a bowl that catches the water? Because they play in the playground themselves, children will be able to offer ideas to explain why different ages of children play in particular places.

Teaching ideas

Using visual resources

Collect visual resources that show examples of patterns:

● Calendar photographs may show fields, hedges and woodlands that form different patterns in different places.

● Aerial photographs show street patterns in towns and cities.

● Estate agents' details contain photographs of many types of homes. These can be sorted into various patterns, for example detached, semi-detached and terraced houses.

● Simple weather records taken over time in school will begin to show patterns in temperature, rainfall and wind direction.

● Road accident information from the local road safety officer will show patterns of what types of accidents occur and where.

Patterns and processes are closely tied in with cause and effect. Use real-world opportunities to help children understand that very few things in the world are clear cut: a volcano can be dormant for hundreds of years and suddenly erupt.

Encourage children to think about patterns and processes in the future. Will towns and cities keep on growing across the countryside forever? Would they want this to happen? Such enquiries link very well with citizenship and develop thinking skills.

Processes

Subject facts

Geographers are interested in processes because they help us to explain how the world is changing. Like patterns, they can be a physical process or human activity. Let's look again at rivers. Water in a river anywhere in the world cuts into the land below it and at the edges. But what takes place as the river flows that leads to the distinctive pattern is the *process*. It moves silt, soils, pebbles and other materials downstream. These also help to erode the landscape. As the water loses energy, it deposits what it has been carrying. These are just some of the many processes that happen in all rivers. It may also help to think of processes as actions that can eventually form the patterns we see across the planet.

Weather

We can look at many processes happening to explain how weather patterns occur all over the world. Huge masses of warmer and cooler air are constantly moving around the planet. They bump into each other and swirl around. Hot and cold air follow certain patterns and, as they move, create the various hot and cold **fronts** we see on the weather maps. If certain conditions arise, special weather processes occur, for example hurricanes. Examples of these will be examined later in this chapter (see pages 79–81).

Human activity

Processes are constantly taking place because of human activity, for example the destruction of tropical rainforests. There are many reasons for this process of destruction, such as the need for grazing land, commercial logging and so on. But the process does not end there. The process of deforestation has an effect on other processes on our planet. There is evidence to suggest that it is affecting the global patterns of climate that can be identified. It can also affect economic processes, for example consumer awareness of the need to understand where products have come from and how their consumption has a knock-on effect in other places.

At the beginning of the 21st century, geographers can identify specific processes taking place in some towns and cities in Britain. Places such as Cambridge and Swindon have developed **economies** based on high-tech and high-value industries and research. This has led to large increases in the workforce who are attracted by high salaries and opportunities in rapidly growing fields. This in turn is leading to dramatic rises in the cost of housing and increased traffic congestion, while decreases in environmental quality are taking place.

Tourism is growing rapidly on a global scale. The World Tourist Organisation estimated that there were about 842 million international travellers moving around the world in 2008. This process contains many other processes. For example, people try new types of food and drink and then place consumer demands to have them available in their own country. This can change agricultural processes in other countries. Tourism changes some of the processes by which disease spreads as people travel more and to a wider range of places. Aids, malaria and avian influenza (more commonly known as bird flu) are three examples.

Why you need to know these facts

Children in both KS1 and KS2 need to develop a knowledge and understanding of geographical processes. By developing an understanding of processes, children gradually begin to learn that the world is constantly changing.

Vocabulary

Deforestation – the felling of trees and clearance of land for other uses.
Erosion – the removal of material by natural (for example wind) and human (for example walkers) means.

Hurricane – a tropical storm with winds of more than 120km/h, created when depressions spiral over warm seas.
Process – the way in which the environment is changed by a series of events.
Tourism – the movement of people to places beyond where they normally live and work, for recreation and leisure.

Common misconceptions

Physical and human processes may not always be separate. If sufficient walkers stray off marked footpaths, they can change the nature of the soil and vegetation over which they travel.

Handy tip

Working models are an excellent way of demonstrating changes in the landscape. They can give the impression of speeding up time. A sand-tray river model (see Figure 5) shows how a river changes its direction and the surrounding land.

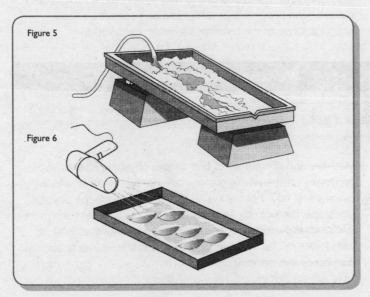

Figure 5

Figure 6

A tray full of dry sand can show how sand dunes are formed and moved by placing an electric hairdryer on a low setting to one side and allowing the flow of air to travel over the sand (see Figure 6 on page 77). School health and safety regulations must be strictly adhered to if attempting this.

Teaching ideas

Speeding up time

Use ICT to help children to observe processes at work. A digital video recording of a river model can be played back at fast speed to give the impression of speeding up time.

Predicting patterns

Repetition of experiments can help children to understand that patterns can be predicted. Take the sand dune model (see Figure 6 on page 77) and place a large pebble in the centre. Start the hairdryer, and video the event. Repeat the process with larger and smaller pebbles and children will begin to understand the similar processes that occur and may be able to predict what might happen if they varied the experiment. This can eventually lead them to understand the link between patterns and processes, by which repeated processes can produce some of the patterns we see in our world.

Weather and climate

Subject facts

Weather and climate affect human and physical patterns and processes on the whole planet. For example, weather affects farming and how homes are built. Weather affects the physical landscape, for example in areas of heavy rainfall, rivers are more common and erode the landscape more heavily than in areas with lower rainfall. Weather also causes extreme events, such as hurricanes and flooding.

Weather studies can help children to understand the links between people and their physical world.

The difference between weather and climate

Weather and climate affect people all over the world, but what is the difference between them?

The word *weather* is used by geographers to describe what is happening in the **atmosphere** at a certain place during a certain time, for example: *The weather today in this part of Lincolnshire is sunny, dry and cool.* The word *climate* is generally accepted as referring to what happens in the atmosphere in a certain place during a period of at least 30 years: *The climate in Lincolnshire is generally considered to be relatively mild and rainfall tends to be lower than in other parts of the UK.*

What makes weather patterns?

Weather and climate are a result of patterns and processes that take place in the atmosphere. The atmosphere is made up from a mixture of gases, solids and liquids. The gases are nitrogen (78 per cent), oxygen (21 per cent) and argon (0.9 per cent). In addition, there are trace gases, such as carbon dioxide, helium, methane and ozone. Solids like soot, ash and dust are also present due to human activity, for example industry, and natural processes, such as volcanic eruptions. Water vapour is also present.

The atmosphere absorbs energy from the Sun. Carbon dioxide, methane and water vapour are good at absorbing this energy. About half of this energy is absorbed by the Earth itself. Nearly a quarter is used to power the water cycle, also known as the **hydrological cycle**. Only one per cent is needed to power atmospheric and ocean currents, while just under a third is reflected back into space. So what causes weather to change? Why isn't it constant?

There are seven main factors that affect the type of weather patterns that occur at any place on the planet:

1. *The prevailing winds.* If you study weather maps on the television or internet for a few days, you will soon see that there is a pattern in the winds that send **air masses** across the British Isles:

- Northerly winds are cold and wet.
- North-westerly winds are cold and wet.
- Southerly winds are hot and dry.

- South-westerly winds often bring in warm, wet weather from the Atlantic.
- Easterly winds can be cold and dry.

However, if you look on satellite television or the internet for the weather in central Germany, you will see a different pattern because more of the prevailing winds have travelled across large expanses of land, compared to those we receive in the British Isles, which have mainly crossed oceans. Therefore, the weather in Germany tends to be more extreme than in Britain, with warmer summers and colder winters.

2. *Latitude.* Places near the equator get more heat for two reasons. The first is because the same amount of energy is concentrated on a smaller area of land. The second is that the energy has to travel through less atmosphere near the equator than it would towards the poles.

3. *Aspect.* In Britain, the northern side of your home will probably be cooler than the southern side. This is because the Sun (when it shines!) warms the southern side. What would be the warmest side of your home if you lived in New Zealand? (The northern side because the Sun is shining from the opposite direction in the southern hemisphere.)

4. *Altitude.* The air becomes thinner at higher altitudes. This stops it retaining heat. As a consequence, the temperature drops by about 1°C for each 100 metres above sea level.

5. *Distance to the sea.* Water needs more energy than land to warm up. But once it gets warm, water keeps the heat for longer than land. This tends to make land warmer than sea during the day, but this reverses by night. As a result, seaside locations tend to be cooler during the day but warmer at night.

6. *Seasons.* In the northern hemisphere, the Sun is more directly overhead during our summer. This tends to make days warmer and brighter. In winter, the Sun is less directly overhead and so less heat is received in the atmosphere and on the land surface.

7. *The greenhouse effect.* It is likely that this topic will be raised at some point in your teaching. However, it's a complex area and the experts are not entirely sure about what is happening. What are the main facts?

- Some gases in the atmosphere absorb the radiation that has arrived on Earth and is being reflected into space. Carbon dioxide, CFCs (chlorofluorocarbons) and methane are very good at trapping this radiation. This gradually heats up the atmosphere.

- Carbon dioxide is increasing because it's made when humans burn **fossil fuels** like coal, oil and gas. Deforestation by fire is especially dangerous because burning trees releases carbon dioxide and at the same time trees that are good at turning this gas into oxygen are removed.
- Methane is increasing rapidly in the atmosphere. Wetlands and paddy fields are an important source of this because stagnant water releases methane through biological activity. Increased melting of Arctic tundra is also releasing additional methane into the atmosphere.
- CFCs are artificial chemicals contained in many of the products we use today, such as aerosols and fridges. They destroy the ozone layer as well as being very good at absorbing the radiation reflected from the Earth's surface. The ozone layer is in fact a zone in the stratosphere high above the Earth where ozone that can absorb the Sun's ultraviolet radiation is present in large quantities.
- The Earth also goes through natural cycles. There have been many glacial periods in the Earth's history. These can change the amounts of greenhouse gases in the atmosphere. This is one reason why it is hard to know whether human influences are the main cause of recent rises in temperature, or whether this is part of a much longer natural cycle.

Violent processes in the atmosphere

These can cause large-scale damage. Hurricanes develop over tropical oceans and start as small depressions in places where sea temperatures must be more than 27°C. Their force comes from the fact that they are trying to move huge quantities of heat to higher altitudes.

The most powerful storms possible are tornadoes. The Great Plains in the mid-west of the USA suffer many of them. As different types of air rush towards each other at high speed, they begin to spin and twist together. A vast sucking effect is created at the centre of the tornado. This draws up objects from the Earth's surface at speeds of up to 100mph (160km/h) and causes severe damage. Heavy rains come with tornadoes and these add to the damage by causing flooding.

Why you need to know these facts

Patterns and processes often explain why things happen on our planet. For example, places with regular patterns of hot, dry weather can become holiday destinations. Understanding patterns and processes can help children to explain what they find in their geographical enquiries.

Vocabulary

Aspect – describes whether a slope faces north or south. In the northern hemisphere, south-facing slopes are warmer than north-facing slopes. The opposite is true in the southern hemisphere.

Climate – average weather conditions for a particular place.

Greenhouse effect – the trapping by the atmosphere of long wavelength heat waves from the Earth's surface.

Tornado – a whirling funnel of wind.

Water cycle – the process by which water evaporates from the sea, creates clouds and falls again as rain and snow.

Weather – what is happening in the atmosphere at a given place and time.

Handy tip

Use children's everyday experiences to develop their knowledge and understanding of geographical patterns and processes. Keep examples simple.

Teaching ideas

● Be familiar with the whole geography scheme of work for your school. You can then refer back to work done earlier to help children to see patterns and processes. For example, if they made weather records in Year 2, you could refer to these when looking at the local micro-climate in Year 6.

● Many of the patterns and processes explained in this chapter take place around the world. Keep alert for opportunities to build them into your geography teaching. This helps to take children beyond their immediate surroundings and into the wider world. In particular, severe weather around the world is often focused on by the media, so children will be aware when instances occur. For example, when a hurricane occurs in the USA, record the news item or find online footage of it, show it to your class, ask them to find its position on a world map and discuss how people are affected by natural hazards that nobody can control.

Ecosystems

Subject facts

Ecosystems are a way of explaining the relationships between animals and plants within the living and non-living environment. Ecosystems can be small, for example the school nature pond. They can be large, such as a whole area of tropical rainforest. Sometimes they appear to have clear boundaries, such as the pond, but even this can be blurred if we think of things that may arrive at the pond from other places.

Thinking about small or large parts of the world as ecosystems can help us to understand the patterns and processes within them. We can learn more about the world if we try to tease out the inter-relationships between animals and plants within the live and non-living parts of their environment. The living parts of an ecosystem are called the *biotic elements* and include things such as plants, fish and human beings. The non-living parts are called *abiotic elements* and include water, rocks and atmospheric gases.

Food chains and food webs
Some living organisms are able to change sunlight into food energy and are called *autotrophs* or *producers. Consumers* are the organisms that live off other organisms. *Food chains* in ecosystems

are used to describe and explain how food is moved within the system in a line. For example, sheep eat grass and in turn humans eat sheep. But it's not always that simple! Foxes will eat some sheep and a few may be killed by dogs, and in turn they decompose, returning nutrients to the soil. This is called a *food web* and helps us to understand just how complex it can all get. Food webs are processes taking place in the natural world and we can use them in geography to help to explain what we observe.

Nutrient cycles

The example above also helps to explain another important concept in ecosystems – nutrient cycles. Keeping it simple, if you never add organic or artificial fertilisers to your vegetable patch, crop yields will decrease. Heavy rain can also have an effect, as it will force some minerals down into deeper layers of soil where roots cannot reach them.

Succession

This is another useful process to consider. What would happen if you left your vegetable patch to nature? Weeds would appear; some crop seeds would germinate and come up another year; the wind and birds would bring in new seeds that would germinate; wind and weathering would blow the soils and debris over the plot. Gradually a whole new range of species would grow on your vegetable plot. If the plot was in southern Spain, eventually a range of species that can survive in those climatic and soil conditions would develop. However, if your plot was in the Midlands in England, a quite different range of species would eventually develop. Given long enough under present climatic and soil conditions, it would become an oak woodland, because this species is ideally suited to the British climate and soils.

Biodiversity

Finally, *biodiversity* must be considered within patterns and processes. The word means the range of all the species of plants, animals and micro-organisms that are found on the planet. It can be thought of in two ways. *Species diversity* means the range of living things in any one place. In gardening terms, consider how many plants, insects and birds live in your garden. *Ecosystems diversity* looks at the range of links between species in a given place. In your garden, this would mean looking at how the range of plants supports butterflies and other creatures that naturally eat the insects that cause damage to plants. The pattern of butterfly distribution in the garden will be affected by the location of plants that attract them. Growing more of these particular plants may create a process by which more butterflies are attracted to the garden.

Why you need to know these facts

Studying ecosystems and biodiversity at a simple level in primary school can help children to understand how patterns and processes work on the Earth.

Vocabulary

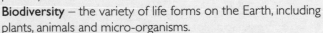

Abiotic – parts of the environment that are not living – water, atmosphere, nutrients.

Autotrophs – green plants, or producers, that use water, carbon dioxide and energy to make carbohydrates through photosynthesis.

Biodiversity – the variety of life forms on the Earth, including plants, animals and micro-organisms.

Biotic – the living parts of the environment.

Ecosystem – the inter-relationships between plants and animals and their environments.

Nutrient cycles – the way elements are absorbed by plants, returned to the environment, and re-absorbed.

Succession – how a group of plants gradually changes in an environment in order to make fullest use of the prevailing conditions.

Amazing facts

Estimates suggest that there are up to 30 million species of living organisms on Earth. As of 2010, only 1.7 million species had been identified by scientists.

Common misconceptions

While we are increasing our knowledge and understanding of patterns and processes on our planet, we still have very few explanations that are complete. For instance, we are not sure of the extent to which global warming is the result of human activity or a complex mixture of this along with natural processes over which we have no control.

Handy tip

Use the school locality as your main resource for teaching knowledge and understanding of ecosystems and biodiversity.

Teaching ideas

In-depth study

Select a small area of your school grounds to study in depth. Try to plan the use of this area so that children will return to it as they progress through the school. Keep thorough records of what is found and the changes taking place. This will help children to build up a small model of how places change. It will help them to understand the causes and effects of patterns and processes. For example, if they create a small pond, they will see how the number of animal species may increase in the surrounding area. The process of creating the pond will lead to new distribution patterns of species and demonstrate the links between pattern and process. If you plant some buddleia bushes, they will attract a wide range of butterflies into the vicinity.

Population

Subject facts

Geographers are interested in populations because they are linked with many patterns and processes taking place on Earth. This section will look at some of the main ones.

Population distribution

The population of the world is not evenly spread out over the planet. There are many reasons for this. The main one is that not all parts of the world are useful for growing food. Greenland, for example, is not likely to see huge increases in population! But some places, such as the fertile river valley of the Ganges, attract many people because food can be grown there. Sometimes, more people are attracted than the land can sustain. For example, the number of **nomads** in the Sahara Desert has increased in areas where vegetation and water supplies are decreasing due to global warming. This has led to the small supplies of vegetation being taken too quickly to allow sufficient time for it to grow again.

A fresh water supply is also very important. This needs to be available all year and must be sufficient not only for food needs but also for other human activities such as food processing, waste disposal and economic activity.

Natural hazards also play a part in where people live. Areas of regular flooding are often avoided, for example, especially as they can be connected with the potential for disease. However, it's not quite so simple as this: farmers will cultivate fields close to active volcanoes where the local soil conditions are good for crops; Tokyo has grown rapidly over the last 60 years, despite it being accepted as a major earthquake zone. The landscape is constantly changing: if sea levels rise as predicted during the next 30 years, communities in coastal areas, such as Bangladesh and the east coast of England, are in danger from severe flooding.

Migration

People have moved across the Earth for thousands of years. Migration is a process with many causes. Some people choose to move because they think life holds better prospects elsewhere. The thousands of rural migrants who arrive in Mexico City are an example of this process. Others move because they believe school prospects for their children will be better in another place. Others migrate for a limited period and then return to their home region. For example, some British workers migrate to Scotland and work in the oil industry before returning to their home area.

Migration also occurs because people are forced to move. The ethnic cleansing and oppression in the Former Yugoslavia during the 1990s is an example of this process in action. It can also occur where major changes in the physical environment force people to move. This can happen for physical and human reasons. For example, the Fukushima nuclear disaster in 2011, which followed a devastating earthquake and **tsunami** in Japan, forced thousands of people to migrate due to radioactivity. Extensive lava flows from volcanoes can also force communities to migrate due to permanent loss of agricultural land.

Population growth

Patterns and processes in population growth are studied by geographers to help to explain what they see happening on the planet. Look at these world population figures:

1800	1 billion people
1960	3 billion people
2000	6 billion people
2012	7 billion people

According to the UN Population Division, the world population could be 8.3 billion in 2030. However, population is not growing everywhere, as these figures, taken from the 2009 World Bank data for national percentage population change, show:

Qatar	9.56%
Afghanistan	2.66%
Cuba	0%
Georgia	−0.83%

These processes can result in various patterns that can be identified. Countries with relatively easy immigration procedures are targeted by people wishing to leave their homelands. Globally, a pattern can be seen of people moving into urban areas. In England, as decaying central areas are redeveloped, the new dwellings are often targeted at more affluent people who wish to live near city centres for ease of access to work and leisure facilities.

Why you need to know these facts

Your children will study localities inhabited by many different people. They need to understand some of the reasons why they are there and what they do.

Population changes occurring in places that you study will vary from place to place. Part of your own background research should try to identify what is happening and why.

Vocabulary

Earthquake – a violent shaking made by sudden movements in the Earth's crust.
Migration – the movement of people around the world. It takes place over short and long distances.
Volcano – a mountain or hill that contains a hole in the Earth's crust through which hot, liquid rock and gases flow.

Amazing facts

The population density of Australia is 6.4 people per square mile. The population density of Singapore is 17,275 people per square mile.

Common misconceptions

People tend to stay where they are.
It is incorrect to think that people stay in the same place. Young children may not have sufficient experience to understand that people move around the Earth all the time.

Teaching ideas

Migration or moving house

Starting with parts of the population such as the children's own families or individual members of the class, you can begin to teach children about how and why people move. Ask questions such as *Has an aunt moved? Who joined the class since September? Where did they come from? Why did they move?* Clearly, sensitivity and knowledge of the families will be needed.

If the local shopping centre has shopkeepers from many parts of the world, look for opportunities to find out where they came from, when their families arrived and why they came. Again, there are sensitivities to be taken into consideration, but careful planning should produce interesting enquiries that will help children to understand why and how people migrate in various patterns around the world.

Your locality may have special examples of migration. For example, if you teach in Milton Keynes, some families may have relocated there because their employers moved out of London. This is where your local knowledge can be a real help in planning geographical work.

Settlements

Subject facts

People live in many types of settlements, located in various patterns.

Rural settlements

Rural settlements can be dispersed or nucleated (see Figure 7 on the following page). A dispersed pattern would be seen when individual farms and buildings are scattered over a landscape. Nucleated settlements have the buildings close together.

There will be patterns within this broad distribution. Where the landscape cannot support agriculture, few buildings will be found, but a line of farms or houses may be seen where springs flow from the hillside.

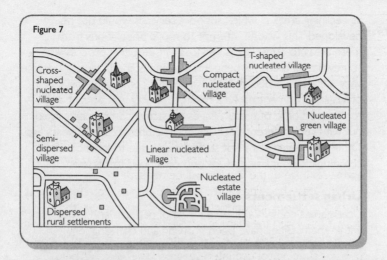

Figure 7

Rural settlements form a range of patterns. Some grow up around a village green, while others spread out along a straight road. This is often seen in the English Fenlands. Many villages now contain a range of street patterns. Old village streets and lanes are often clustered around the village centre (which quite often includes features such as a church or a pub), while new street patterns can be seen where estates of houses have been added to the village.

The rural population is changing and this is affecting settlements. The processes taking place are normally linked with developing patterns of migration. The Cambridge region has already been mentioned (see pages 60 and 76). With the rapid growth of high-tech employment opportunities in the region, housing costs in nearby villages rose rapidly and put pressure on green-belt land. Places that were once left as wasteland suddenly became valuable. For example, the pattern of building on former air bases has resulted in the development of large artificial villages within commuting distance of Cambridge. The settlement of Cambourne, to the west of Cambridge, is an example of one type of new development appearing across England as a response to growing housing demand. A government-proposed eco town to the north of Cambridge is also being considered.

Other patterns can be identified elsewhere in Britain. As the coal mining industry declined for various reasons in the north-east of England, local authorities designated some villages as declining areas in which support services would not be developed. This was an attempt to move populations from these areas to consolidate services. The resulting process was somewhat different. As property values declined, housing became very attractive, especially as it was within commuting distance of larger urban centres. As a result, property was bought and renovated. Some of these villages are active communities again, but with very different population structures to, say, 50 years ago. Others, however, were not so fortunate, due to location and communication infrastructure, and continued to decline.

Urban settlements

Urban areas contain a diverse range of patterns and processes within them. Cities have been growing and changing for thousands of years. Today, they are interesting for the way that they are being adapted to rapid changes in technology, society and employment.

Geographers often develop models to offer explanations about why we see certain patterns and processes in our towns and cities. Of course, each one place is unique, but it's fascinating to see the extent to which many of the processes shown in models can be seen on the ground.

Many city models were developed in the USA, but Mann's model was specifically designed for UK towns and cities (see Figure 8).

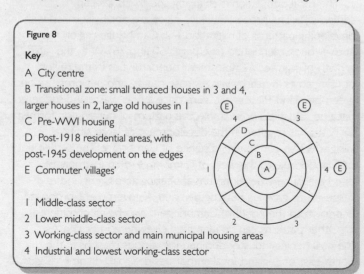

Figure 8

Key

A City centre

B Transitional zone: small terraced houses in 3 and 4, larger houses in 2, large old houses in 1

C Pre-WWI housing

D Post-1918 residential areas, with post-1945 development on the edges

E Commuter 'villages'

1 Middle-class sector

2 Lower middle-class sector

3 Working-class sector and main municipal housing areas

4 Industrial and lowest working-class sector

This model is based on the idea that most UK towns and cities developed during industrial growth in the 19th century. The prevailing winds in the UK tend to be from west to east. This resulted in most industry being located in eastern parts of cities and towns. Workers lived near to their employment, while richer people tended to settle in the cleaner western areas of these towns and cities. It sounds simple and it did occur in many places. Once geographical processes start, they are difficult to alter. Deliberate planning and redevelopment can change this. For instance, the docklands area of London has encouraged the movement of city employees into areas they would not previously have considered. However, when these processes do occur, land and property values increase and this in turn forces some sectors of the population into other areas.

Issues of environmental sustainability also exist within patterns and processes in towns and cities. For many years, they grew as suburbs developed as a result of growing affluence in some sectors of the population and changes in transport technology, such as the growth of the London Underground. Planners saw urban areas growing out of control and introduced green-belt policies. Today these are being challenged, especially in the south-east, as a result of growing demands for land for building houses. However, much inner-city land is derelict. A pattern that has been developing in UK urban areas is for this land to be used for redevelopment. Many government schemes have been formed to manage these projects: Urban Development Corporations, Enterprise Zones and the London 2012 Olympics regeneration project. Evaluations vary as to the success of these initiatives.

Why you need to know these facts

All children live in settlements of some form. Familiarity can lead to making assumptions that 'everywhere must be like this'. Therefore, a study of settlements can help children to understand the similarities and differences between them.

Vocabulary

Derelict – land damaged by industrial processes and neglect, and so unsuitable for further use unless it is adapted.

Dispersed settlement – a pattern of rural settlement where people live in scattered farms and houses.

Green belt – an area of land surrounding an urban area that has strong planning rules to limit development on it.

Nucleated settlement – a rural settlement where buildings are closely grouped together.

Rural settlement – small groups of buildings in the countryside.

Urban settlement – a large area of built-up land.

It should be remembered that there are no universally accepted definitions of *rural* and *urban*.

Amazing facts

At the start of the 21st century, half of the world's population lived in cities. By 2008, more than half of the world's population lived in cities.

Common misconceptions

We use the terms *urban* and *rural* almost without thinking. However, specialists are not agreed on definitions for these terms. The issue is made more complex by developments in ICT that allow people to do jobs in rural places that 20 years ago were mainly done in cities. Different countries have different classification systems: settlements in Iceland with more than 2000 people are called urban, but in Japan only settlements with more than 30,000 people are described as urban.

Teaching ideas

Your school locality
Walk your school locality to really get to know the settlement it is in. Even if you live there, you'll be surprised at how much you take for granted until you look really carefully. Get to know the local people, especially those who have lived there a long time.

A different locality
Make links with a school in a settlement quite different from the one that your school is in. Use ICT to link the children and exchange information.

Pattern detectives
Find a street plan of your town and ask children to be 'pattern detectives' and mark where they think different types of roads and streets are. For example, they may get a clue from streets which are all named after lakes in the Lake District. This also links the locality to the wider world and develops geographical knowledge.

Land use

Subject facts

Looking at land use shows a wide range of geographical processes and patterns taking place. It's useful here to keep a sense of scale. We can look at land use across the whole of the UK or focus on a small locality.

The Geographical Association co-ordinated a national survey of land use in 1996. Rex Walford in *Land Use UK* gives a very interesting analysis of patterns and processes that are occurring at the present time. But what are the underlying processes that affect land use?

Physical environment
Let's start with the physical environment. The underlying rocks in any place will affect the shape of the land, the drainage and the

quality of the soils. These in turn will affect the type of farming that can be sustained. Some physical environments can be changed. Once the Fens in East Anglia were drained, they enabled the land to be used for agriculture. This huge flat area is even more attractive today as it encourages an industrial approach to agriculture, with field sizes increasing to make farming even more cost-effective. Hilly land with steep slopes doesn't encourage arable farming as it's difficult to use modern machinery in such conditions.

Climate

The location of any place will be affected by the climate in that region. The warming effect of the Gulf Stream helps to make the south-west of Britain attractive both as a tourist region and retirement area. East Anglia has a mild and dry climate, but with sufficient rainfall to enable very productive arable farming to take place. The climate patterns that exist in these areas have encouraged particular processes of agriculture and tourism in each area.

Relationship to other places

The location of a place in relation to other places is key. The city of Milton Keynes was deliberately located halfway between London and Birmingham. Planners saw it as a way of collecting together the predicted growth of housing and employment in that region. Land was relatively cheap and good communication routes already existed through the region. Planners intended the inhabitants to work in the employment zones within the new city. This is happening on a large scale, but, because of good communications and much higher property prices nearer London, many inhabitants of Milton Keynes commute to London each day. On the other hand, the north-east of Britain continues to have difficulty attracting and maintaining a strong employment base. Although a skilled workforce exists, the distance of the region from larger population centres in the south-east and Europe is affecting sustained growth. However, new technology can decrease the effects of location and distance: many telephone call centres have been established in the north-east as they are not dependent on physical links and geographical distances. So we can see a process occurring, based on developments in ICT, that is creating a growing pattern of employment around the country.

Historical links

Layers of the historical past can also affect land use processes. Tourist 'honey pot' destinations such as Stratford-upon-Avon and York draw on their historic and cultural links to develop specialised forms of economic activity. There is a heavy concentration of cultural and historic land use in the southern region of Britain. To enable some of this economic activity to be spread across the country, new attractions such as the Royal Armouries in Leeds (**www.royalarmouries.org**) and the National Glass Centre in Sunderland (**www.nationalglasscentre.com**) have been established. Only time will tell as to whether their locations away from the south-east will secure their long-term viability. On the other hand, it has been argued that difficulties in gaining easy and cheap transport access to the Millennium Dome in London was one reason for its limited success. A central location may not be the only factor affecting land use – excellent communications and cultural commitment are also important.

Technology

Changes in technology also affect land use patterns and processes. The London suburbs began to expand rapidly as the underground system spread out into the countryside. It is argued that high-rise building in city centres really became viable as lift technology developed. Increases in private car ownership enabled people to live further from their place of work. However, with an estimated 31 million cars on British roads in 2010, geographers pose the question about how long this pattern can be sustained. As more jobs can be conducted using information technology rather than workers being in a particular location, home-working is a rapidly growing situation. This may have long-term implications for land use in traditional areas containing office buildings. Also, as more people work at home, the demand for services in residential areas will change.

Why you need to know these facts

Looking at how the land is used can help children to focus clearly on what is happening in a place and start finding explanations for it. This is central to effective geographical enquiry.

Vocabulary

Land use – what an area of land is used for, such as farming, factories, car parks.
Gulf Stream – warm currents of ocean water from the Gulf of Mexico.
The Fens – large, flat areas of land, mainly in eastern England, that were once under the sea before being drained.

Amazing facts

Approximately ten per cent of the global population lives in the southern hemisphere. This places large pressures on land use in the northern hemisphere.

Common misconceptions

Children find it hard to understand that the world is constantly changing. For example, the land on which their school is built may have been farm land 20 years ago. 300 years ago, it may have been woodland.

Handy tip

Have a look on this website to find excellent photos from all over Britain showing how the land is used: **www.geograph.org.uk**

The Geographical Association's journal *Primary Geographer*, Number 70 (Autumn 2009) contains a wide range of ideas for carrying out land use studies. Go to the Geographical Association's website to find out how to join and about all the excellent resources they provide: **www.geography.org.uk**

Tectonic patterns and processes

Subject facts

The Earth is constantly on the move, not just through space but also inside and on the surface. This is called **plate tectonics**. It's a theory to describe and explain some of the physical patterns and processes observed on Earth.

The Earth's crust

As long ago as 1620, Francis Bacon observed how the land masses on each side of the Atlantic Ocean could be fitted together. Since then, more research has provided evidence to suggest that the continents are moving around the surface of the Earth. There are a number of theories offered to explain what is happening. They all work on the idea that the temperature rises as you travel towards the centre of the Earth. Rather like the current of heat in a boiling saucepan, this heat is moving around inside the Earth and heating and cooling its various layers. Continents are huge slabs of rocks 35–40km thick. They travel across the Earth's mantle. The heat currents cause them to move towards each other in some places, and apart in others. Continents collide and, when the edges cool, they get heavier and sink back into the mantle (see Figure 9 on the following page).

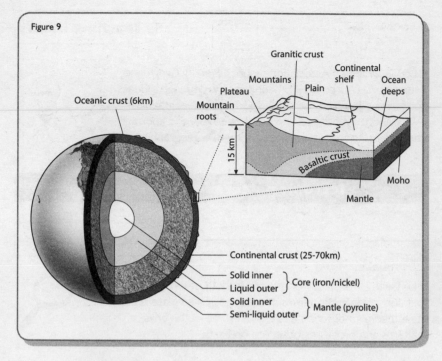

Figure 9

Volcanoes

All this activity results in a number of physical processes. The huge power produces faults and folds in the rock that make up the Earth's crust. Where the crust is weak, molten ash and lava can reach the surface through various types of volcano. Some volcanoes explode through a hole in the crust and send out large quantities of lava and ash. Others are much less violent and send lava spreading out across the landscape, causing different types of damage.

The processes of these active volcanoes create different dangers for humans in the vicinity. Lava flows destroy and submerge buildings and farmland. Gases and acid rain can fall in the area if lakes have formed in the crater prior to the eruption. Pyroclastic flows send out, at high speed, rock and ash that in large quantities cause damage and suffocation. Eruptions can start mudflows that damage and ruin property.

There are over 500 active volcanoes in the world and many of them produce a specific location pattern. The one shown by the dashed line in Figure 10 is called the Pacific Ring of Fire.

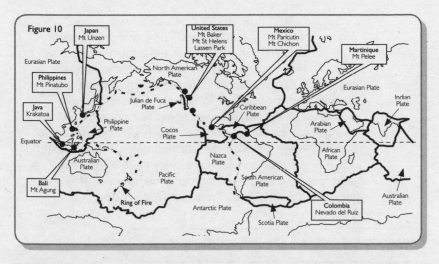

Figure 10

Earthquakes

Earthquakes occur along a range of plate boundaries where large-scale movements take place. This ring is also the location for many of the world's earthquakes. The huge pressures that build up where plates meet cause violent shaking of the ground. The magnitude of earthquakes is measured according to the Richter Scale. The intensity is measured on the **Modified Mercalli Intensity Scale**.

Modified Mercalli Scale	Richter Scale	Earthquakes per year
<III	<3.9	830,000
IV to V	4 to 4.9	62,000
VI to VII	5 to 5.9	500
VIII to IX	6 to 6.9	100
X to XI	7 to 7.9	20
>XII	>8	>0.5

<III	Slight movements, rather like a passing truck.
IV to V	Felt by everyone; windows and dishes broken.
VI to VII	Fallen plaster; chimney pots broken; slight damage.
VIII to IX	Damage considerable; underground pipes broken.
X to XI	Foundations cracked; rails bent.
XII	Total damage.

Earthquakes cause various types of damage. Land movements destroy buildings and communication systems such as roads, and services such as electricity are disrupted. Fires can break out, causing damage after the earthquake has ended. Earthquakes can also trigger landslides and avalanches that cause further damage. If the earthquake occurs under the sea, tidal waves and tsunami can develop. Tsunami are especially violent as they begin from the ocean bed. The waves are not especially high when in deep water and they are often not seen until very close to land. Even after these events, danger can occur because decaying bodies can spread disease that in turn can kill survivors.

Why you need to know these facts

Children cannot fully understand the world if physical processes and patterns are not investigated. Also, they often ask questions about what they see and hear happening around the world.

Vocabulary

Famine – very limited or no supplies of food for a population.
Lava – rock that comes out of volcanoes – some is runny, some is viscous, while some is shot out in the form of volcanic 'bombs' or lumps of rock.
Mantle – the layer of the Earth below the crust.
Modified Mercalli Intensity Scale – a means of allowing witnesses to use their observations to say how strong an earthquake was.
Plate – part of the Earth's crust that moves across the Earth.
Richter Scale – a way of measuring the energy released during earthquakes.
Seismometer – a device for registering the size of earthquakes.
Tsunami – a huge tidal wave, normally started by an earthquake or volcano.

Amazing facts

Scientists are getting better at predicting volcanic eruptions. Mount St Helens is a huge volcano in the USA. Since its first huge event in 1980, 19 of its 22 eruptions have been accurately predicted. It was classified as active again in 2008.

Common misconceptions

Earthquakes only happen in other countries.
In fact, small tremors are regularly recorded in various parts of Britain and sizeable tremors have been known. The 2008 tremor centred on Market Rasen in Lincolnshire had a magnitude of 5.2.

Handy tip

Use television and other media to collect images and reports of natural events around the world. Build up your collection so that you always have materials available to help answer children's questions.

Teaching ideas

Earthquakes
● Children can simulate how shock waves from earthquakes move by spreading sand along a plank of wood and hitting the end of the plank with a rubber hammer (you must ensure that this is carried out safely). The sand nearest the hammer moves more violently than that further away. This shows how a shock wave is strongest near the epicentre (start) of the earthquake.
● Access the BBC news website for first-hand accounts of recent earthquakes: **www.bbc.co.uk/news**
● Seismometers are used to register earthquakes. Get children to devise ways of registering, and perhaps recording, sudden movements in the classroom. For example, can they create a

simple device that picks up a slamming door, traffic thundering past the school or movements across a wooden classroom floor?
● If you can get there, the Science Museum in London has an excellent earthquake simulation area. See the museum's website for details: **www.sciencemuseum.org.uk**

Weathering

Subject facts

Weathering is the term geographers use to describe how rocks are broken up. There are three main types of weathering: mechanical, chemical and biological.

Mechanical weathering

There are five types of mechanical weathering: freeze-thaw, disintegration, pressure release, salt crystal growth and weathering by wind.

● *Freeze-thaw weathering.* This happens to rocks in places where the night and day temperatures vary considerably and there is also a lot of moisture. Water seeps into cracks and holes in the rocks during the day. When the water freezes during the night, the expansion of the water forces pieces of the rock to break off.

● *Disintegration.* This happens in desert areas where it's hot in the day and cold at night. The heat makes the rock expand and the cold forces it to contract. This builds up pressures in the rock and outer layers are shattered off.

● *Pressure release.* If rocks have been subject to huge amounts of pressure, for example when under a glacier, the release of pressure when the cause is removed makes the rocks crack, causing pieces to break away.

● *Salt crystal growth.* Where temperatures regularly reach around 26–8°C, rocks with high salt content are cracked because some salt crystals expand by up to three times in high temperatures. This causes pieces of rock to break off.

● *Weathering by wind.* Wind can also weather rock over long periods of time. This is best seen in areas with soft rock. Old buildings made of sandstone sometimes have amazing wind-carved surfaces, where wind has smoothed the rock over hundreds of years.

Chemical weathering

This occurs most effectively underground where there are large quantities of water. Limestone and chalk can be weathered, causing caves and underground tunnels to form.

It can also occur in atmospheres where industrial chemicals eat away at exposed rock surfaces, both in natural places, such as cliffs, and on buildings made of rock.

Biological weathering

This happens when plants and animals break down rocks. Roots pushing into cracks and burrowing animals are two examples. Human activity, such as mountain biking, can also weather rock surfaces. Moss and lichens growing on exposed rocks can have a weathering effect. They tend to appear on north-facing surfaces and help to demonstrate the importance of aspect and slope on weathering processes.

Why you need to know these facts

Weathering is one of the processes that makes the world a constantly changing place. A basic knowledge of how weathering takes place will help children to develop their understanding of how change occurs.

Vocabulary

Biological weathering – when rocks are worn away by plants and animals.
Chemical weathering – when rocks are worn away by chemical reactions.
Mechanical weathering – when rocks are worn away by physical processes such as disintegration.

Amazing facts

Huge temperature ranges in desert areas can make rocks shatter. This is caused by stresses building up in rocks that reach 40°C during the day but can experience near-freezing temperatures at night.

Common misconceptions

Weathering is only caused by natural processes.
This is not the case. People weather the landscape too: walkers wear down landscape around footpaths; factories emit chemicals that can rot rocks and building materials.

Teaching ideas

Weathering at school
Practical experiments help children to understand how weathering takes place. Get them to find examples around school: grass areas that have lost the grass through people taking short cuts; doors where the paint has been removed by constant scuffing; paint blistering and falling off woodwork that gets direct sunlight (compare this with woodwork in shaded areas).

Soils

Subject facts

Soils are very important to humans as they provide the environment for much food growth. They are made up of living and dead organic materials, weathered bedrock, water and air. They form very slowly and there are very many different types. The soils in any one place will depend on the bedrock, what is growing at the surface, the angle of slope, the aspect of that slope and the amount of water that either falls as rain or seeps through the soil from other places.

We need to know the texture of a given soil to work out some of its properties. By looking closely at the size of the particles in a soil sample, its make-up and properties can be found. An easy way to do this is to take a soil sample big enough to fill one-third of a transparent container with a screw top lid. Fill one third of the volume of the container with clean water, screw on the lid and shake vigorously. Leave the contents to settle, ideally over a period of weeks. Ask children to carefully record the layers of sediment as they build up. The various particles will separate out, with the largest and heaviest making a layer at the bottom. Eventually, a layer of the finest silt will settle on the top of your layered sample. Repeat this using samples from various locations.

It is interesting to look at **soil horizons**, but bear in mind all the health and safety issues such a study entails. If a trench is cut into soil, the horizon is revealed. This can be seen when digging trenches for pipes or foundations. In many places the horizon contains a mixture of natural and human features. Such a study interests the geographer and the archaeologist. In more remote places, cutting a soil horizon will reveal natural processes. Bear in mind that **soil profiles** in the school grounds will not be natural as builders' activity will have mixed up the layers (horizons) and probably brought in new materials.

Why you need to know these facts

The patterns and processes described here will be taking place in many of the areas you study with your pupils. This introduction is designed to increase your confidence in answering children's questions and to help you to develop enquiries that will extend your knowledge and that of the children. For instance, where can children find examples of the three types of weathering around the school? Can they then go on to explain why they occur in those places?

Vocabulary

Bedrock – the rock directly beneath a layer of soil.
Silt – very fine sediments deposited by slow-moving water.
Organic – describes material that was once or is still alive.
Particle – small piece of rock, vegetation or sand material.
Soil feature – the size and range of particles in a soil sample.
Soil horizon – a soil profile normally contains three horizons. The A horizon may be considered the topsoil. The B horizon is material that is undergoing change through various processes. The C horizon is broken up material made from the bedrock.
Soil profile – a vertical cross-section of soil.

Teaching ideas

Soil tests

Is the soil in each flower bed in the school's grounds the same? Conduct soil tests and find the best places to grow particular plants. This could include looking at micro-climates and showing how many features in the environment are linked.

Resources

Useful reading

'Focus on extreme Geography', *Primary Geography,* Number 76 (Sheffield: Geographical Association, Autumn 2011).

Land Use – UK. A Survey for the 21st Century by Rex Walford (Sheffield: Geographical Association, 1997).

Hot Topics: Weather and Climate by Peter Riley (Scholastic Ltd, 2012).

Hot Topics: Habitats by Peter Riley (Scholastic Ltd, 2012).

Class visit

Visit the Science Museum in London, where many practical activities will help children to understand the physical patterns and processes explained in this chapter. See the website for details: **www.sciencemuseum.org.uk**

Teaching resources

● Images of natural events – recorded television or online reports on earthquakes, newspaper cuttings, and so on.
● Rock samples.
● Soil samples.
● Building materials.
● Old maps and plans that show change in the locality.
● Old photographs, drawings and engravings.
● **www.bbc.co.uk/schools/websites/4_11**

Chapter 4

Environmental change and sustainable development

Effective environmental education contains a balance of three things: education *about, in* and *for* the environment.

Education *about* the environment concerns all the facts that children need to know in order to carry out an enquiry. What happens to water in the landscape and how does it get polluted? How do we use fuels to make electricity? What happens to rubbish when it is collected from your home? What do aerosols actually do to the environment? What does the word **recycling** mean? Why are people protesting about electricity pylons being put up in the countryside?

Education *in* the environment is about planning work that will put children in real-world situations to learn about environmental change and sustainability. It's fieldwork. At a local level, it means investigating how clean a stream is and visiting the sewage works to see what happens there. At a broader level, it means visiting a wind farm during a residential field visit to see alternative technology at work. At a global level, we can do virtual fieldwork via the web: What is happening in other countries to help people use their cars less? Could we use these ideas in our locality?

Education *for* the environment is about providing opportunities for children to become involved in projects that will improve the environment. What can be done in school to use less electricity? What plants could be grown in the school grounds to encourage a wider range of wildlife? It could include looking for opportunities to involve children in community projects, such as helping to recreate a hedgerow in the locality. Education *for* the environment is also about developing a range of values and attitudes.

Local environmental change

There will be many changes taking place in the local environment around your school. Some of these are easy to spot because they have a large impact, while others might be hard to find, but are nevertheless important. For example, the building of a new road is a big event and the effects of the change are easy to see. On the other hand, the materials being discharged from a nearby factory chimney may not be visible to the eye but do affect the environment. As well as the size of the changes, the speed of change can also be important. The gradual decrease in the number of wild flowers and birds in a rural area caused by the use of farming chemicals may take place over many years and be hard to see, but a sudden accidental discharge of chemicals into a local river may make very visible changes to the wildlife in and around it.

Some local changes may be hard to see simply because of familiarity with our locality – because we see something every day, we often take it for granted and either miss the changes or fail to understand the event we are seeing. Let's consider some of the environmental changes that may be taking place in your school locality.

Transport

Local transport can offer many ways of looking at local changes. The number of cars on the roads in Britain doubled between 1970 and 1995, reaching an estimated 31 million by 2012. If you can find some old photographs of your locality they may well show how transport has changed your local environment. A 1950s photograph of your high street may show people quite safely crossing the road with only a few cars visible. The same view today may show a constant stream of traffic with controlled crossings being the only safe way to cross. How can we make this situation more sustainable? Who comes to school by car every day? Do they really have to? Some schools have developed a virtual bus system where carefully supervised groups of children meet up each day and walk to school together. Not only does this reduce the volume of traffic, atmospheric pollution decreases and it can improve levels of road safety.

The example of the virtual bus can also show children how cause and effect can be positive and negative. The effects of ICT can make very interesting enquiries. Most supermarkets offer internet shopping from home. If your local store provides this, why not arrange for children to look into how this affects the local environment? How many people use this facility? Where do they live? How many car miles are saved each week, over a year? How much fuel is saved? Can the children find out the volume of **pollutants** that have been prevented from getting into the atmosphere? On the other hand, how much electricity is needed to run a computer at home and in the store? What fuels do we use to make this electricity and how do power stations pollute the environment?

Waste

Your school can be an excellent place to see environmental change at work. One important way we are changing our world is through rubbish and waste disposal. This links well with sustainability because this theme allows us to study recycling activities and how things are made.

Responding to change

Another important dimension of local change is that it provides opportunities for children to consider how they feel about what they see changing. This leads to thinking about how decisions are made and the effect they can have in developing a more sustainable environment. Change can be positive as well as negative. This balance needs to be watched as you plan enquiries into your changing locality.

What other features in your locality may be changing? This checklist may help you to find them:

● Changes in your school and its grounds, for example making a wildlife area.

● Buildings that are being built, changed or demolished.

● Changes in land use, for example a sports ground being made on a farm field.

● Changes in the services, for example different shops on the high street.

Environmental change and sustainable development

- Changes in the people who live in the locality, such as the building of a sheltered housing complex.
- Changes in environmental quality, for example a sudden increase in vandalism.
- Changes in transport types and patterns, for example more lorries driving through the village.
- Changes to natural features, like the removal of hedges or increasing pollution in a stream.
- Changes in links between the local area and the wider world, such as more people visiting your town as tourists.
- Changes to how the locality feels, for example has a crime prevention scheme made the locality feel safer?

The examples in this section on local change cannot cover everything you will have in your locality. They are intended to encourage and give ideas for how you can use the changes near you in effective planning of your geography curriculum.

Why you need to know these facts

We take our immediate surroundings for granted. Teachers often live beyond the school locality. It's important to look out for changes in the school locality in order to build them into the geography curriculum. Changes often happen slowly and may not be seen easily. Therefore, children need support in developing skills to identify change in the environment.

Vocabulary

Land use – what an area of land is used for, for example factories, farming, car parks.
Pollutants – materials that degrade the environment and have harmful effects.
Waste disposal – the removal of materials no longer required by people.

Amazing facts

You can watch the global population change in real time at:
www.breathingearth.net

Common misconceptions

Change only happens because of what other people do.
A part of effective environmental education is for children to begin to understand that nearly everything they do has an effect on the environment. Each time they flush the toilet, they use water supplies. How much water might they save in one year if a brick was placed in the cistern to reduce the volume of water used for each flush? Do children come to school by car? How much fuel might be saved if they walked to school? Might they be fitter, too?

Change only happens somewhere else.
Change does not only happen in distant places that are reported in the news. Local changes may be hard to spot or simply taken for granted, but they can be just as important as dramatic changes that receive extensive coverage.

Handy tip

● Constantly keep in mind the everyday things we take for granted. Use them to study changes in the local environment. What new species of bird now visits the school courtyard since specially chosen shrubs were planted? Why is the local play park being vandalised more frequently? Is internet shopping at the local supermarket cutting down pollution from cars in local streets?
● Collect and file local photographs, maps, newspaper cuttings, video recordings and comments from people living in the school

locality. Over time, these will build up into a bank of excellent resources to show just how quickly and intensively a small area does change.

Teaching ideas

Recognising changes in the environment

Children in KS1 should be taught to recognise changes in the environment. They also have to learn how the environment may be improved and sustained. You can use the seasons to help children to understand that some changes happen in patterns and sequences. Find a camera that you can use for an entire year. Ask your class to choose a view of the school grounds that they like. Arrange for children to photograph the same view each week for a year. Perhaps the caretaker could do this in the holidays? You will end up with 52 very useful images that clearly show how the same place changes over time. Some will be natural, such as the changing colours of leaves. Others will be human, for example the arrival of a seat or bench.

Sustaining the environment

As well as showing the changes, the photographs could also be used to get the children to think about how the place shown could be improved and sustained. For instance, they may spot that the grass is getting worn away because short cuts are taken across it, causing it to be untidy. How could they solve the problem? Ask them to draw what the same view might look like if they came back in 5, 10 or 50 years. This will help them think about how we can sustain our environment. There are good children's fiction books which illustrate how our world changes that will support this work. Try:

● *Window by Jeannie Baker (published by Walker Books, 2002)*
● *Belonging by Jeannie Baker (published by Walker Books, 2008)*

Waste disposal

Discuss packed lunches. If children bring these to school, set up an enquiry into how much rubbish these generate during a day.

Taking full account of health and safety issues, ask children to bring their packed lunch boxes into the classroom after lunch.

Get them to sort all the waste materials into groups. Weigh each group. Find out how much space it takes up. Can it be crushed? If this is one day's waste, use a spreadsheet to work out the weights and volumes for a week and the school year. When the waste goes to the tip, what will decompose and what will stay the same? Bury samples in controlled places for different lengths of time so that children will see the effects of time and natural processes on waste materials. Lead on to questions of sustainability: *How could packed lunches be made in order to reduce the amount of disposable rubbish?*

Measuring change

At KS1, get children to investigate how they change. Keep records of height, weight, favourite toys (be aware that these can be sensitive issues). Involve them in taking simple weather recordings for a week. Even a short time can demonstrate how the environment changes. Take photographs out of the classroom windows. Build up an image timeline display beside each window and ask children to spot any changes they see.

At KS2, keep weather records over longer periods to begin to show seasonal changes in temperature, hours of sunshine, rainfall and so on. Study photographs of the school grounds taken over a number of years and ask children to identify changes and explain why they may have occurred. Encourage children to think about whether they like or dislike the changes they find.

Global environmental change

Subject facts

The global environment is constantly changing. As with local events, these can be natural processes or initiated by people. Some can be a mixture. This section will outline the major environmental changes taking place on our planet.

Climate change

The world's climate was changing even before human beings could make any impact upon it. There is growing evidence that human activity is having an effect, but experts are not entirely sure about the extent of this or the way it interacts with natural climatic changes that would still happen if we were not here.

Global warming is one example of climate change. The Earth warms up because energy from the Sun reaches it, is absorbed by the planet and retained in the atmosphere. However, changes in the gases that make up the Earth's atmosphere have meant that more and more energy is being trapped. Since we have been burning fossil fuels such as coal, oil and gas, the amount of carbon dioxide in the atmosphere has risen. Carbon dioxide contributes to trapping energy in the atmosphere. CFCs are found in fridges and aerosols, which gradually release them into the atmosphere. They trap energy. In fact, per molecule, they are 10,000 times better at it than carbon dioxide.

But we must be careful of oversimplifying the issue. It may be interesting to explain to children that these processes change naturally: we have evidence of an 11-year solar cycle that causes the amount of energy reaching the Earth to vary. Also, global temperatures are changed by other things: deforestation and **desertification** are changing the extent to which the Earth's surface can reflect energy. Ocean currents are changing. This affects their heating and cooling of the planet. Volcanic eruptions can also change global temperatures. Researchers offer a number of effects that global warming may create in the future:

- More warming may take place at the poles than at the equator.
- Prevailing winds will change.
- Levels of rainfall will change, with continental places becoming drier.
- Sea levels will rise.
- There will be changes in ice cap size and shape.

The ozone layer

Only a tiny part of the Earth's atmosphere is made up of ozone, but it is very important. Ozone helps to stop the Sun's ultraviolet light, called UV-B radiation, from reaching the surface of the Earth. This radiation is one cause of sunburn, skin cancer and eye cataracts. Recent research is providing evidence that increased UV-B radiation can reduce yields in some crops. The hole in the ozone layer over Antarctica was discovered in 1982 by scientists from the British Antarctic Survey. It changes in shape and size. In 2011, the ozone hole covered an area of 25 million

Environmental change and sustainable development

square kilometres, larger than its average size over the previous decade. The hole has developed because more and more CFCs are present in the atmosphere. These have been used since the 1930s in refrigerators, cooling systems, aerosols and some plastics. They are complex chlorine compounds and set up chemical reactions that destroy the ozone. Once present, it is estimated that CFCs take 100 years to break down. While more developed countries are now reducing their use, industries in the developing world are increasing their output of CFCs. The impact of changes in ozone protection affects people, animals and crops throughout the world.

Population change

At a global scale, the population is changing in a number of ways. World population is increasing.

Global population	
1960	3 billion
1974	4 billion
1987	5 billion
2000	6 billion
2012	7 billion

According to the UN Population Division, the estimated world population for 2030 is 8.3 billion and it is 9.6 billion for 2062. However, the changes have more complex patterns within them, so we have to be careful when using this area in our teaching. The population in many developed countries is now decreasing. Some developing countries, many of which are in the African continent, still have high rates of population growth.

If we look at the structure of a country's population, we can see other **demographic** changes. The numbers of people of various ages changes over time. For example, Russia is currently experiencing a decrease in young people due to a falling **birth rate**. However, the number of older people is increasing due to a variety of factors, including better standards of health. But this too can be a generalisation. There are regional variations on these trends. In the UK, for example, men and women in the north-east of England tend to die at younger ages than those in some other areas of the country. A growing number of adults in the UK live alone. This in turn affects the demand for certain types of housing.

It is unlikely that you will go into such depth with children at KS1 and KS2. However, do be alert to ways in which these changes may be seen in your locality or other places you study. For example, why is there extensive provision of sheltered housing in your locality and how can we help older people with different needs? A study of another country may show differences in the roles of men and women that could lead to enquiry about the effects of education and the values held by people around the world.

Changes in population migration

Human beings have always moved around the Earth. They move for different reasons:

- *Exploration*. People move to find new sources of food and shelter. Sometimes this is permanent, but it can also be seasonal, for example nomads who move animals to food sources as the seasons change.
- *Famine*. This can be caused by natural events, such as **drought**, or when brought on by over-farming.
- *Natural disasters* like earthquakes, floods or volcanoes.
- *Disease*. People may flee from areas that endanger health.
- *War*. People either want to get away from fighting or are forced out by processes such as ethnic cleansing.
- *To improve the quality of life*. The huge growth of Mexico City is an example of rural dwellers perceiving life to be better in an urban environment.
- *Family ties*. Sometimes one member of a family migrates and relations follow.
- *Seasonal migration*. An example of this is people who work abroad in tourist areas for part of the year.

It may be possible to find examples of these migration patterns taking place in one of the localities investigated by your pupils. However, issues such as immigration are sensitive and need to be approached professionally, ideally through a whole-school procedure.

Deforestation

According to the Food and Agriculture Organization of the UN, 13 million hectares of forest were converted to other uses

annually between 2000 and 2010. This is an area equivalent to
the size of Costa Rica. Most deforestation occurs through forest
fires. These occur for a number of reasons:

- *Natural causes.* Lightning can start them. It is estimated that
100 strikes hit the Earth every second.
- *Land clearing.* The forest is deliberately burned to provide land
for agricultural use.
- *Timber demand.* Trees are felled to accommodate the huge
global demand for wood. Often some timber is burned to get
around environmental laws.

These causes account for a huge number of fires, mainly
in Brazil, Colombia, Africa, Indonesia and New Guinea.
Deforestation has various effects on the environment:

- *Local and global climate change.* The amount of forest affects
the ability of the planet to reflect the Sun's energy.
- *Carbon dioxide levels.* Trees absorb carbon dioxide. Fewer trees
on a global scale is one factor contributing to increases in carbon
dioxide in the atmosphere. This in part promotes global warming.
- *Soil in the deforested area can change.* Once the forest
has gone, some soils quickly become unsuitable for any
other purpose.
- *Rivers change.* The increased run-off from the land changes
their characteristics.
- *Loss of wildlife.* Tropical forests contain huge numbers of
wildlife species. Research suggests that some of these could
provide medical benefits to humans. Deforestation can mean the
permanent destruction of such global resources. However, natural
forest fires and controlled burning can encourage new and
healthy vegetation growth.

Urbanisation

It is estimated that during the 1990s the global population swung
from being mainly rural to mainly urban. Urbanisation is one of
the largest changes taking place on the planet. The pattern of this
change varies around the world. The most urbanised continent
is South America. Europe, North America, Australia and New
Zealand are also highly urbanised. Seven of the world's ten largest
cities are in developing countries: Mumbai, Mexico City, São
Paulo, Manila, Shanghai, Jakarta and Karachi. The highest rates of
urbanisation are occurring in the developing countries. A number
of reasons have been offered by geographers to explain this:

- Developing countries want to join the global **economy**.
- Cities offer effective economies of scale for industry. They locate industries close to each other, keeping transport costs down.
- Cities contain large labour forces.

However, cities are very complex places. To be effective, they need many services. Water, electricity, sanitation, drainage, health and education services, and transport systems are all needed to ensure the success of a city. They need to provide space for people to live healthily and in safety. One of the biggest environmental problems facing the planet is that these resources are underdeveloped in the world's largest and fastest growing cities. This leads to high levels of pollution and poverty. The pace of environmental change is huge in these cities. Their growth changes the rural areas surrounding them. Fewer people are available to work in farming. Waste from the cities is dumped in surrounding rural areas.

Environmental change caused by global urbanisation will continue to grow. It is a complex process, but, with so much of the world's population affected by it, children need some introduction to the main issues at primary school. You may wish to consider developing an enquiry into a locality in one of the cities mentioned above.

Some recent research provides evidence that counter-urbanisation is taking place in advanced countries like the USA, New Zealand, Sweden and Great Britain, which are highly urbanised. City inhabitants who are sufficiently wealthy move further away from the city to live in what are perceived as more attractive rural areas. Some cities in advanced countries now show declines in population.

Why you need to know these facts

Global changes help to explain some of the changes that you and your pupils will find locally. A longer-term aim of environmental education is to develop children's understanding of the connections and patterns of cause and effect that happen around the world.

Environmental change and sustainable development

Vocabulary

CFCs – synthetic chemicals that can destroy ozone.

Deforestation – the destruction of forest due to the felling of trees and clearance of land for other uses or by naturally occurring forest fires.

Desertification – degrading of land in arid, hot areas by natural and human processes.

Global warming – a climate change caused by the build-up of greenhouse gases that absorb long-wave radiation from the Earth and return some back to the Earth.

Ozone layer – gas in the atmosphere that filters out harmful ultraviolet radiation.

Seasonal migration – the temporary movement of people for work and agriculture.

Urbanisation – the expansion of towns and cities.

Amazing facts

- More and more people around the world are infected by malaria because of huge increases in global travel. Malaria now kills nearly 3 million people each year.

- It is estimated that up to ten per cent of the British population moves address each year, causing extensive changes in many parts of the country. Who are the new children and adults in your school this year? Where have they come from and why did they move?

Common misconceptions

Global warming means that the British climate will get warmer.

Recent research into the effects of ice melting in the Arctic suggests that our climate could get colder, as the cold water from melting ice may prevent the Gulf Stream from maintaining its warming effect.

Handy tip

When planning work on global change, look carefully at the resources and sources children will be using. Aim to provide a balance of viewpoints. Look for positive changes as well as often-quoted and more easily found negative ones.

Teaching ideas

Use videos
Search the internet for recordings of the news items and programmes on global changes that are often broadcast. Show small sections of these to extend children's locational knowledge and awareness of global issues. Get this approach built into your whole-school geography policy to develop effective progress and continuity.

Predict the future
Ask a class what they think the world will be like in 5, 10 and 15 years' time. Why do they make these predictions? What would they like to happen in the future? How do they think they might change it? There are links here with citizenship and health education – how we can work with other people to maintain a healthy environment.

Make a survey
Survey your school to find out what part it is playing in global change:
● Are lights and other electrical appliances switched off when not needed?
● Is waste paper recycled?
● Are the cleaning products used environmentally friendly?
● What happens to biodegradable waste, such as grass cuttings from the school field and lunchtime waste?
● Is the school well insulated? How might the insulation be improved?
● How do children travel to school? Could fewer car journeys be made by sharing transport or developing a community virtual bus?

Sustainable development

Subject facts

Sustainable development is a relevant term for geography programmes of study at KS1 and KS2. The 1987 Brundtland Report contains a widely quoted definition:

> *Development which meets the needs of the present without compromising the ability of future generations to meet their own needs.*

The 1993 Sustainable Development Education Panel offered this definition for teachers:

> *Education for sustainable development enables people to develop the knowledge, values and skills to participate in decisions about the way we do things individually and collectively, both locally and globally, that will improve the quality of life now without damaging the planet for the future.*

In order to define sustainability further, some geographers – see *The Environment* by Chris Park (Routledge, 2001) – refer to a list of nine principles of sustainable development:

1. *Respect and care for the community of life.* The *community* of life is an attempt to sum up what we know about ecosystems and balance in nature. A practical example of this would be the use of natural methods for controlling pests in a garden.

2. *Improve the quality of human life.* The desire to improve the quality of human life should be seen on a global scale. At the moment, about 20 per cent of the human population consumes about 80 per cent of the resources. About 80 per cent of the population consumes 20 per cent of natural resources. The statement aims to recognise that, somehow, we should be working towards sharing the world's resources more evenly.

3. *Conserve the Earth's vitality and diversity.* The Earth's vitality and diversity refers to the idea that when nature takes its course, a wide range of species create amazing, self-supporting

environments. For example, the wildlife of Antarctica has a harsh existence, but in spite of this penguins and other creatures live in a successful balance together.

4. *Minimise the depletion of non-renewable resources.* Many of the Earth's resources are non-renewable. This statement asks us to consider using alternative resources. Do we urgently need to consider much greater use of solar and wind power to generate the energy we need?

5. *Keep within the Earth's carrying capacity.* The carrying capacity of the Earth is a way of thinking about how much any ecosystem can stay the same when we put pressure on it. An example might be the global stock of fish. At present, humans are fishing the world's oceans at a rate that is greater than natural processes of fish reproduction. The result is that stocks are diminishing. If this continues, we will cause permanent damage to global fish resources.

6. *Change personal attitudes and practices.* 20 per cent of the world's population has become used to consuming global resources at a high rate. It is only possible to remain sustainable if individuals reduce their demand on the environment. For instance, we have become used to using tumble dryers to dry our clothes. They use large amounts of electricity and put heat into the atmosphere. Clothes on a clothes line use natural energy from the Sun and wind to dry and have almost zero impact on the environment. But, with our present lifestyles, this is sometimes perceived as inconvenient and inefficient. Personal attitudes and practices may need adapting to ensure a sustainable future.

7. *Enable communities to care for their own environments.* Individuals by themselves may feel rather powerless to develop more sustainable ways of life. An emphasis on community is seen as a way of empowering people to work together on sustainable development projects. A simple example of this is car sharing to get to work. It requires organisation, but can reduce traffic congestion and environmental pollution.

8. *Provide a national framework for integrating development and conservation.* It is important to work at national levels, with a particular emphasis on public policy to encourage more sustainable ways of life. Following on from the previous example, at present we do not have an integrated public transport system in England. The present networks rarely encourage us to use public transport, hence the increase in the number of private cars on our roads. Changes here need to be tackled at a national level.

9. *Create a global alliance.* Many groups and organisations are currently attempting to forge a global alliance in which all countries accept the need to co-operate in developing more sustainable ways of living. This principle meets head-on the realities of current global issues and is not easy to achieve. The use of CFCs is one example. They are cheap and the developed world has used them for about 70 years. Now we understand the damage caused to the atmosphere, we are using more sustainable but more expensive alternatives. People in the developing world want the same products but do not have the resources to use the more expensive versions. Hence there is concern that levels of CFCs in the atmosphere may be very hard to reduce as more and more of the global population demand products that contain them. Should developed countries provide support to enable the developing world to use more sustainable technology?

The future

It could be argued that there are three key points on sustainable development that now need discussion:

● *Inter-generational implications of patterns of resource use.* How effectively do decisions about the use of natural resources preserve an environmental heritage or estate for the benefit of future generations? This requires us to ask hard questions about the future. How long can we continue to use the world's resources without considering the needs of future generations? A practical example of this can be found in how we generate energy. Nuclear fuel is used around the world to generate electricity. It produces waste radioactive products that we have to dispose of. Although we attempt to dispose of them safely, in reality we do not fully understand the degree of safety achieved by the process – we may be leaving a dangerous legacy for future generations. We have technology available to replace nuclear power stations with wind and solar electricity generation. These solutions would also leave a legacy for future generations, but the effects on the environment may involve much less risk.

● *Equity concerns.* Who has access to resources? How fairly are available resources allocated between competing claimants? An interesting example of this comes from the world of satellites and computers. Since the 1990s, the USA has been operating a satellite system for remotely sensing the location of minerals. Other countries are now using similar technologies to do the same thing. Traditional surveying methods are expensive and time consuming. With global natural resources becoming depleted, any country with the technology and knowledge to find new sources clearly has a considerable advantage. It also places them in a position of power relative to other nations. Satellite technology is also being used to locate new stocks of fish and fresh water around the globe. Will nations use this new knowledge for their own benefit only or might it be shared with other people?

● *Time horizons.* How much are resource allocation decisions oriented towards short-term economic gain or long-term environmental stability? Tropical rainforests are being destroyed for a number of reasons. The majority of these are to enable either commercial organisations or governments to benefit from short-term economic gain. Developing countries are striving to become part of the global economy as they perceive this to be essential for survival. Competition is fierce and computer technology and communications make change very rapid. Economics play a dominant role in global activity. Politics, economics and environmental change are tightly connected. Are current environmental programmes sufficient to counter these trends?

Why you need to know these facts

It is important to teach children knowledge and understanding of environmental change and sustainable development, and to encourage them to ask questions about important and sometimes controversial issues. These raise important professional considerations.

What do we teach?
● Do we just provide the facts and leave children to make up their own minds?
● Do we present information about the environment as though it is black and white and clear-cut?
● How accurate is the information we use with children?
● What perceptions do children bring with them to school?
Martin Ashley in *Improving Teaching and Learning in the Humanities* (Routledge, 1999) describes the example of a London primary

school child who explained to her dad that he would have to take down his greenhouse because of the effect it had on the environment.

● What impact will the environmental work you do with children actually have on their ideas and actions?

Environmental education is not just about facts and information. It is a process we offer children to help them begin to understand how the environment is changing and how human beings interact with it.

Vocabulary

Pollution – placing materials in the environment that damage natural processes.

Resources – can be natural (for example coal), human (for example an ICT-literate workforce) or capital (for example an office building).

Solar power – energy harnessed from radiation from the Sun that falls onto the Earth's surface and atmosphere.

Common misconceptions

Experts know what is happening in the changes we can see taking place on Earth.

In fact, there is only limited agreement on the many questions we have about what we see happening. As we discover more, we have to adapt our explanations and predictions. We need to bear this in mind when working with children to avoid them developing misconceptions about the world.

Questions

Are ideas and questions about the environment too complex for primary children to be exposed to?

There is little research evidence to support or refute this question. However, by introducing children to the environment and sustainability through their own experiences, we can create some foundations for extending their knowledge and understanding of and interest in the future of the environment.

Teaching ideas

Get inspired by these ideas, then do some research into what initiatives are currently going on in your school locality and what's available for you to develop.

● Do a survey with the children to find out how many of them cycle to school. You may find the numbers are low. Look into why this is. Maybe the routes are not safe enough or the bicycle storage facilities are insecure? You could think about working with the local authority to find ways of making cycle routes safer for children.

● Maybe you could get your electricity from a wind turbine in the school grounds? Having a turbine on site provides children with first-hand experience of alternative energy sources.

● Surplus paint from DIY stores, that would otherwise be thrown away, could be used to improve open spaces at your school such as playgrounds, car parks or other municipal areas.

● Get involved in a sustainable woodland programme, or similar. Look at the Woodland Trust's website for information: **www.woodlandtrust.org.uk**. Children could learn how woods work and develop their own woodcraft skills using natural materials from a sustainable source.

● Ask the children to design an environment postcard (or e-card) and look into ways it could be used in county activities.

● Arrange a Walk to School project to initiate work on more sustainable ways of travelling.

● Design and build a giant chessboard, outdoor performance area or courtyard garden to improve the school environment.

● Look at the land around your school and investigate ways of improving community life. For example, if there is open water within the local area you could design water safety activities for the young and old.

● Do you have a piece of derelict, sloping land in your school grounds? You could consider designing an earth sculpture in the shape of an amphitheatre, and get the local community to help create it. You could then use this space for school performances.

● Consider a project to develop the habitats on your school grounds. Maybe you could introduce a wetland area, a wild flower meadow or a butterfly garden?

● Involve the children in building nesting boxes for use in the school grounds and around your local town. This will actively show children how a shared community approach can have a real effect in creating a more sustainable environment.

Each of these examples offers opportunities to explore sustainable environmental education in action and contains aspects of education about, in and for the environment. The good thing about such projects is that you don't always have to work alone. Look into applying for support from local authority workers. This can lead to gaining funding for projects. You could involve local businesses or work with interest groups such as the RSPB (**www.rspb.org.uk**) to enlist specialist help. Be proactive and creative, and use what you have in the immediate environment as your starting point.

Citizenship and PSHE

Some of these suggestions also show how citizenship and PSHE may be planned into work on sustainable development. Improving the local community, involvement in active citizenship and health education are all areas that could be covered using the examples listed in the Teaching Ideas section above.

Resources

Useful reading

Window by Baker, J. (London: Walker Books, 2002).

Belonging by Baker, J. (London: Walker Books, 2008).

'Environmental geography' by Essex-Cater, L. & Rawlinson, S. in *Primary Geography Handbook,* edited by Scoffham, S. (Sheffield: Geographical Association, 2010).

'Focus on sustainable schools', *Primary Geographer,* Number 64 (Sheffield: Geographical Association, Autumn 2007).

The Environment, second edition, by Chris Park (London: Routledge, 2001).

Improving Teaching and Learning in the Humanities edited by Martin Ashley (London: Routledge, 1999).

Hot Topics: Weather and Climate by Peter Riley (Scholastic Ltd, 2012).

Teaching resources

Teaching packs

Environmental Change photopack (Folens)

Thematic atlases

Philip's Wildlife Atlas by Kerrod, R. & Stidworthy, J. (London: Philip's, 1997).

CD-ROMs – KS2

Guardians of the Greenwood (4Mation)

Websites

Envirolink: **www.envirolink.org**

Environment Agency: **www.environment-agency.gov.uk**

Friends of the Earth: **www.foe.co.uk**

The Rainforest Action Network: **www.ran.org**

Worldmapper: **www.worldmapper.org**

Global Footprints: **www.globalfootprints.org**

World statistics in real time: **www.worldometers.info**

GeoHive: **www.geohive.com**

US census information: **www.census.gov/main/www/popclock.html**

Environmental change and sustainable development

Fieldwork equipment

This is a general list of useful equipment (the specific aims of a visit may need extra equipment, for example a river study will need wellingtons, measuring equipment, a water testing kit and so on): clipboards (A3 size makes sketching and writing easier); plastic bags to keep work dry if it rains; a selection of pencils and crayons; compass; binoculars for observing distant features; digital camera; digital audio recorder; stopwatch; simple soil-testing kit; large-scale plans of the area being studied; photographs; tape measures; cloud, tree and pond life identification charts; clinometers; plastic bags to collect samples, of soil for example; local leaflets and directories; quadrats; digital video camera for recording change, interviews and movement in the environment.

Water

Most children enjoy playing with and in water. Quite a few adults do too! As teachers, we can use this natural curiosity and enjoyment to encourage children to learn about water in our world. Geographers have come up with many words and processes to explain the part water plays on our planet. These can be very confusing to children and adults. As teachers, it's important to remember that perhaps the most effective learning will develop out of practical activities, both in the field and in the classroom. The purpose of this chapter is to explain the main facts about what happens to water in our world. It is in three main sections: river processes, coastline processes and human effects on the coast.

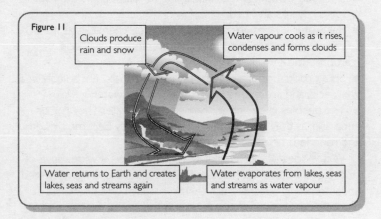

Figure 11

Clouds produce rain and snow

Water vapour cools as it rises, condenses and forms clouds

Water returns to Earth and creates lakes, seas and streams again

Water evaporates from lakes, seas and streams as water vapour

The water cycle

Water is constantly being recycled around the Earth. Water in lakes, rivers, the seas and even puddles is heated by solar energy and evaporates into the atmosphere as water vapour. When the atmosphere cools, water droplets form clouds as the water vapour condenses. Clouds then return water to the Earth as rain and snow. It flows across the Earth's surface and once again creates lakes, rivers, seas and puddles. The whole process is then endlessly repeated (see Figure 11 on page 133).

River processes

Subject facts

A useful list of basic facts – from Liz Lewis in the *Handbook of Primary Geography* (Geographical Association, 2010) – to help us to understand at KS1 and KS2 how rivers work is:

- Water flows downhill.
- Water has the power to carry a load.
- A lot of water can carry more than a little water.
- Fast-flowing water can carry more than slow-flowing water.
- When water slows down, it carries less (it drops some of its load).
- The load is important as a scraping tool, as it helps the river to erode the banks and bed.
- Rainwater is not pure because it picks up chemicals as it falls through the atmosphere and is therefore a weak acid (carbonic acid).
- Some rocks (for example limestone and chalk) are soluble in a weak acid, and are therefore dissolved by rainwater.
- The pebbles in a river are carried by the water. They roll or jump and, as they grind against each other, they become smooth and rounded.

Water does all these things over (and under) a wide range of landscapes. That's what helps to make our surroundings so varied and interesting. But there are certain patterns and processes at work that are repeated all over the world.

River systems

When we study our local stream or river, we are seeing just one part of something bigger. It is important to remember that the bit we see in our local area is part of a much bigger river system comprising many different zones.

Drainage basin

A river system works inside a *drainage basin* – the area of land that provides the water for the river (see Figure 12).

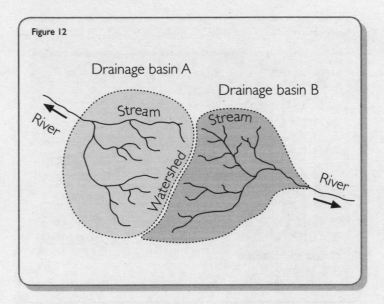

Figure 12

Drainage basin A

Drainage basin B

The boundary of the drainage basin is called a *watershed*. If you imagine the boundary of the basin being like the apex of a house roof, you will get a good idea of what happens: some water flows down one side of the roof, while water falling on the other side flows in the opposite direction. This is what happens on the hillsides along the boundary of the drainage basin. Three main processes take place in a drainage basin:

1. Water erodes a river channel.
2. Water transports materials from upstream to downstream.
3. Water deposits materials to create new landforms.

Figure 12 shows how a drainage basin works as a transfer system to move *sediment*. Sediment means everything from tiny grains of sand to the largest boulders a river can carry. It also includes other things, such as tree roots and other materials like peat from the moors.

Figure 13 on the following page shows what happens in a basin, but it's important to understand that although we highlight particular zones of rivers they are not completely separate features in the real world. At any point along a river, production, transfer and **deposition** might be happening. What the Figure is really saying is that, on the whole, a river produces material upstream and tends to deposit most materials downstream.

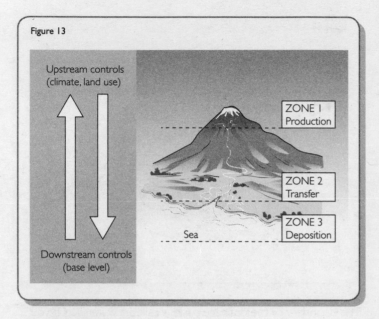

Figure 13

Long profile

The next feature to look at in a drainage basin is the *long profile*. Imagine being able to cut through the landscape like cutting across the diameter of a Yorkshire pudding. If you did this along the course of a river, you would see what its long profile looked like.

The gradient is often steepest in the upstream parts where fast-flowing water is cutting sharp channels into the landscape. As it gets nearer the sea, the river flows much more slowly across wide flood plains. The water flows more slowly because it has lost a lot of energy, is being halted where it meets tidal sea water and because the river channel here is much flatter.

If a river flows across a layer of harder rock, it takes longer to cut through it. This shows up as a *knickpoint* on the long profile. Sometimes a *waterfall* is made where for thousands of years the river has flowed over a layer of hard rock above a softer layer, wearing it away (see Figure 14 on the following page).

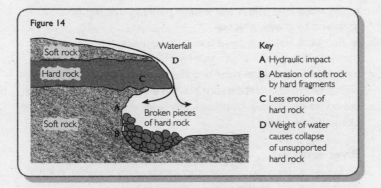

Figure 14

Waterfall

Soft rock

Hard rock

Soft rock

D

C

A

B

Broken pieces
of hard rock

Key

A Hydraulic impact

B Abrasion of soft rock
by hard fragments

C Less erosion of
hard rock

D Weight of water
causes collapse
of unsupported
hard rock

If you look at a map, aerial photograph or satellite image, you'll see that river systems create fascinating patterns across the landscape. These are called *drainage patterns*. The pattern created by nature depends on different things:

- the slopes in the landscape
- how hard and porous the rock is
- faults and joints in the rock
- special shapes in the landscape, for example volcanoes.

Water flow

Water moves in many different ways in a river channel. This is called the *water flow*. Gravity makes water flow downhill. The river channel resists the flow depending on how it is made:

- Very narrow channels force water to move rapidly through them.
- Smooth river beds and banks encourage water to move quickly with less turbulence, while rough surfaces jumble up the water more.
- Straight channels help water flow smoothly. Bends in the channel make the water travel at different speeds.
- Water near the bed and banks travels more slowly than water in the centre of the river or stream.
- The amount of water in a river will change the flow. A lot of rain in the drainage basin will make the river flow more quickly. This gives it more energy to erode and move sediments.
- Humans also affect flow by building weirs, **dams** and bridges.
  The flow of a river enables it to carry a *load*. A river will contain a mixture of three main types of load:
- *Suspended load.* This is made of the very finest particles of silt and clay, which a river holds and carries as it flows along.

- *Dissolved load.* This is the soluble material that has been dissolved by chemical action.
- *Bed load.* This is material that is moved along the bed of the river. This type of load moves in three ways – *rolling*, where particles roll along the river bed like marbles on the playground; *sliding*, where the particles are pushed along the river bed rather like an ice hockey puck; and *saltation*, where sediment is bounced along the river bed.

River erosion

So far, we've seen that water *erodes* sediments from the river channel. But it does this in more than one way:

- *Abrasion.* The river bed and banks are worn away by the load hitting them and physically breaking them up. The load in a fast-flowing river does this more effectively than one that is slow flowing. Heavier and more angular sediment abrades more than light, smooth material.
- *Attrition.* As it moves, particles in the load keep hitting each other. Gradually, they break up into small pieces, depending on how hard the original materials are.
- *Hydraulic action.* Air can get trapped in river water as it flows and tumbles along. The energy in a river can push this air and water hard against the river sides. This can even wear away solid rocks, as the pressure concentrated in small areas is often quite large.
- *Corrosion.* This is also called *solution* and happens when chemical ions, often calcium, are removed by flowing water.

Six aspects of river flow control the effectiveness of erosion:

- *Velocity.* The faster the flow of the river, the more likely it is to erode.
- *Load.* Heavier and more angular contents are most effective at erosion.
- *Gradient.* Steeper gradients, or slopes, encourage more erosion.
- *PH.* More-acidic water increases erosion by solution when it flows over rocks, such as chalk, that can be dissolved by acids.
- *Geology.* Soft rock is more easily eroded than harder rock.
- *People.* Dams, extracting water for industry and building artificial river banks are just three examples of the many ways in which people change the opportunity for a river to erode.

All of this erosion helps the river change its course over thousands of years as it eats away some parts of the land and deposits its load in others. This movement across the landscape is called *meandering*. We are still learning about exactly why and how rivers meander. It is thought that meanders start when a river deposits piles of sediment that it has sorted into fine and coarse particles. These piles have different shapes and start to affect the speed and flow of the water in different parts of the river. This means that the water flow starts to cut into one bank more strongly than the other. Gradually, it changes from being almost straight to having gentle, and eventually much stronger, curves. Some rivers develop broader meanders and the meanders themselves can also move further downstream. Figure 15 shows the development of a typical meander.

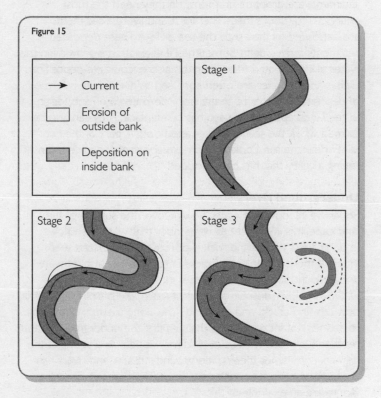

Figure 15

Current

Erosion of outside bank

Deposition on inside bank

Stage 1

Stage 2

Stage 3

The outside bank is steeper because the flow of water is stronger here. It eats away the bank, helping the river to increase its meandering. The water flow on the inside bank is slower. Slower-flowing water cannot carry its load so easily and tends to deposit sediments to make a gently sloping beach. Over time, this builds up and, along with the cutting action on the outside bank, helps the river to change course.

Sometimes the meanders double back on themselves. Because the river is constantly trying to find the shortest and easiest course, it can break through the narrow space between two meanders and cut off a section of the river course. This leaves an ox-bow lake, as shown in Stage 3 of Figure 15 on page 139.

Forming a delta or estuary

Finally, the river will reach the sea or perhaps an inland lake. Its flow is halted and gradually it deposits its load. The heaviest sediments are dropped first because they need the most energy to transport them. The finest and lightest sediments are deposited furthest into the sea or lake. These deposited sediments form a delta. Sometimes, if vegetation is growing in the water at the mouth of the river, this also encourages deposition. Deltas and *estuaries* are often confused. While a delta is formed of deposited sediments, an estuary is formed when subsidence of the landscape near the sea has taken place. They can also be formed when the sea level rises and floods a part of the river valley near the sea. Looking at an estuary gives the impression of seeing a valley that has been flooded.

Underground rivers

So far, we've looked at water flowing over the surface of the landscape. It is important to remember that water also flows underground. Where the rock is porous, rainwater can seep into it. If there are holes or cracks in rocks, these also let water underground. If it finds weaknesses in the underground rock, water can either dissolve the rock, if it is made of soluble material, or it can find cracks and gaps and flow along them. Impermeable rock does not let water pass through it. If the underground water reaches such rock, it flows on and may appear as a spring at the surface. Sometimes these underground streams and rivers can cut huge caverns over millions of years. The caves at Cheddar Gorge are an example of this.

Water also flows through disused mines. Over time, this can weaken adjacent rock. It can also cause a build-up of dangerous chemicals that can then flow out onto the land.

Why you need to know these facts

Many processes take place in rivers. If you hold this knowledge you should be able to identify these when you work with the children on river studies.

Vocabulary

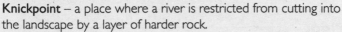

Delta – an area created by sediments deposited at the mouth of a river.

Drainage basin – the area of land that supplies water for a river.

Estuary – a coastal area where sea levels have risen or subsidence has taken place, flooding part of the main river valley.

Knickpoint – a place where a river is restricted from cutting into the landscape by a layer of harder rock.

Meandering – changes in the position of a river's course in the landscape.

Sediment – fine materials carried by a river or stream.

Watershed – an imaginary line dividing the drainage basins of two rivers.

Amazing facts

The River Nile in Africa is the longest river in the world, at 6690 kilometres or 4157 miles.

Common misconceptions

Water can flow uphill.

The only way water can flow uphill is by humans using technology to make it do so. Give children plenty of practical experience with water. Historical studies of Egypt and the River

Nile provide an excellent opportunity for showing how people have invented machinery to move water uphill. Children can design and build their own methods, thus making effective links between history, technology and geography.

Rivers always flow to the sea.

This is not always true. Some rivers flow into large inland lakes. Others have been dammed for people to use the water first and then it reaches the sea through human-built channels such as drains.

Rivers flow directly to the sea.

This is only rarely true. For example, the source of the River Severn is not far from the Welsh coast to the west, but the river actually flows east and south for hundreds of miles before reaching the Bristol Channel. This is because the catchment area slopes away from the Welsh coast.

Questions

Why do some rivers and streams dry up at times?

The most frequent cause is that too little rain falls in the catchment area to feed the river. Sometimes, people take too much water out of the river for farming, industry or use in homes. This can cause a river to dry up or have very little water in it.

Teaching ideas

Wet walks

At KS1, we can start children thinking about river systems by taking them out when it's raining. Get them to observe what happens to rain when it hits something: it rolls down sloping roofs; it disappears into drains; it soaks into some soils; it forms puddles in the playground – it's on the move. Ask them to think about where it has come from and where it might be going to. That will introduce them to the idea of a river system.

Create a drainage pattern

You can show children river drainage patterns easily by putting a couple of bags of sand on the playground. Get them to make hills and valleys, press some parts very firmly, mix earth with sand in some places and push pieces of wood into the sand to simulate harder rock. Then ask them to sprinkle water over their landscape using a watering can. Very quickly, lots of different drainage patterns will appear in their landscape, created by the varying properties the children put into it.

Water flow can be modelled in a simple way by using a piece of wide guttering about 150cm long. Line it by gluing sheets of sandpaper on the concave surface, leaving one area of smooth plastic. Lift one end using a brick to give a simple river profile. Place sand and small and large pebbles at the raised end. Try to find a mixture of smooth and angular materials. Gently pour water into the raised end and watch how the water transports the sediment (see Figure 16).

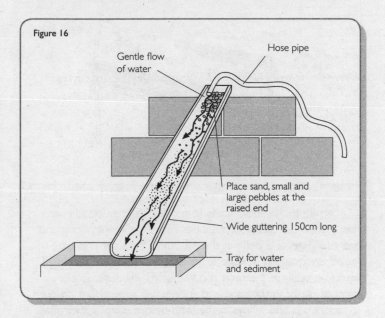

Figure 16

Gentle flow of water

Hose pipe

Place sand, small and large pebbles at the raised end

Wide guttering 150cm long

Tray for water and sediment

Children will see how the sediments move in different ways. They can offer their own explanations. Changing the gradient and water flow will produce different results. Before doing this, ask children to predict what might happen, and why they think so. This model can be used very successfully at KS1 and KS2 by modifying the number of variables you build in: children might experiment with different types of sand or use muddy water.

One of the most useful river models uses a sand tray. This one has an open end to allow for the water to flow out naturally (see Figure 17). By placing pieces of wood under the sand at the upstream end, the angle of slope can be varied. You will need to be able to control the flow of water into the river, to create an even flow. A very effective way to do this is to fill a home brew beer barrel with water. These have taps at the base that give you excellent control over water flow. A piece of rubber tubing connected at one end to a tap will also work. Control the flow by attaching a large bulldog clip at the other end. Don't have the water turned on strongly as it will create too much water pressure.

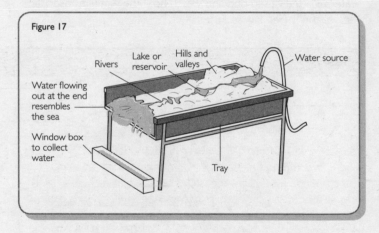

Figure 17

A gentle trickle soon starts to model features found in real rivers. It will cut channels, meander, move sediments along and eventually create a delta at the mouth of the river. This type of model is extremely flexible, for example: place small pieces of wood vertically in the sand and waterfalls will develop; bury a sheet of plastic in the sand and springs will appear. Get children to model hills and valleys in the sand before starting their river. Ask them to put model houses where they think they will be safe from the water. This is an excellent way of encouraging children to make predictions about what may happen when the water starts to flow.

Really good model rivers may take a couple of hours to develop, but there's not usually time to watch this long. To overcome this you can:

● give groups set times for two-minute observations to see how the model has changed since their last visit. If they have a simple plan of the sand tray, they can record in different colours where the river is at each observation.

● set up a digital video camera to record the river model over a two-hour period. Then play the video on fast forward. This will be like watching a river change over thousands of years and very effectively shows children that the landscape is changing even though it can be hard for us to see.

A river model can also show how a river erodes, transports and deposits a load. Allow the children to look closely at the grains of sand being moved along by the water. They will see the processes explained earlier in this chapter. A hand lens can be very useful here.

Coastline processes

Subject facts

Coastal areas are constantly changing. But what actually is the coast? In some books the term *littoral zone* is used to mean the places on Earth where coastal processes take place and create specific coastal features. Coastal areas are where these features interact:

● the sea
● the climate
● rivers reaching the sea
● the geology of the land by the sea
● biological activity both in the sea and on land
● human processes.

Time is another important factor to keep in mind. Some coastal processes take millions of years, for example the gradual deposition of sediments in the delta of the River Nile. Others happen very quickly, such as the floods on the east coast of England in February 1953.

Waves

Waves are made by the wind blowing across the surface of the sea. There are two main types of wave:

● *Swell waves* form far out at sea and can travel a long way.
● *Storm waves* only travel short distances and are created by local winds near the coast.

As waves reach the shore, they are slowed down by the friction of the seabed. When a wave hits the beach, it moves up it. This is called the **swash**. As it loses energy, the water rolls back into the sea due to gravity. This is **backwash**. *Constructive* and *destructive waves* have different effects:

● *Constructive waves* help to build up beach materials. The swash of these waves is greater than their backwash, resulting in them pushing sand up the beach. These waves are normally made by the swell caused by storms happening far out to sea.
● *Destructive waves* hit the beach and cut it away, moving sand into the sea. These waves have backwash greater than their swash. They are mainly caused by local storms and winds close to the coast.

When waves hit the shore at an angle, they can move sand along the beach. This is **longshore drift**. It's not always an even process because the coast is not straight. *Groynes* are used along some parts of the coast in an effort to control this movement of sand through longshore drift (see Figure 18).

Figure 18

Groyne

Beach

Sea

Beach

Groynes

Material accumulates on the side of the groyne facing the direction of longshore drift

Longshore drift

Tides

Tides occur at regular and predictable times. They are created by the effect of the gravitational pull of the Moon on the water in seas and oceans. The Sun's gravitational pull also has a small effect. There are three types of periodic tide:
- *High spring tides* happen when the Sun and Moon are aligned just after a full Moon.
- *Low spring tides* happen just after a new Moon.
- *Neap tides* happen when the Moon and Sun are at right angles to the Earth.

The shape of the coast, the ocean basins and weather conditions can also alter the tides along the coast.

Tidal range means the difference between the height of low and high tide. Enclosed seas, such as the Mediterranean, have very small tidal ranges. In places where the incoming tide is forced up funnel-shaped channels, a *tidal bore* is made. This happens in the estuary of the River Severn.

In some parts of the world, severe storms can raise sea levels and cause *storm surges*. When air pressure drops, sea level rises. The effect is increased where funnel-shaped coasts exist. This often happens in the Bay of Bengal where the River Ganges reaches the sea in Bangladesh. It's a very heavily populated area and storm surges cause great damage to property and loss of life. In 1970, more than 300,000 people were killed as a result of one surge.

Coastal erosion

The coast is eroded by a number of different processes:
- *Abrasion.* The sea carries materials as it moves. When waves hit the coast, this material wears away the cliffs by breaking pieces off the coastal landscape.
- *Solution.* Where the coast is made of rocks such as limestone acidic water can gradually dissolve the rock.
- *Quarrying.* The sheer force of sea water pounding away on the coast can help erode the coastal landscape. As with river erosion, the air that gets compressed by the tumbling waves can also erode the surface as it is suddenly released.
- *Attrition.* As pieces of the coast break off, they tumble against each other. Gradually the pieces are broken down, making them easier to transport along the coast or out to sea.
- *Human factors.* Run-off from hard surfaces, such as roads and car parks, can add to erosion caused by natural processes.

● *Freeze-thaw weathering.* When sea and rainwater freezes in cracks and joints in rocks, it expands. This increases pressure on the rock which can then break off.

● *Biological weathering.* Burrowing creatures can weaken coastal structures. In some areas even sponges, molluscs and urchins can break down coastal features.

As these erosion processes take place, landslides and slumps further weaken the coast and change its shape. Coastal areas with faults and weaknesses in the rock erode more quickly. Hard rocks such as granite wear away more slowly than soft rocks like clay.

All these processes help to create a range of coastal features. Figure 20 gives you starting points for identifying these during fieldwork and while using secondary sources, such as photos.

When cliffs are eroded by the sea, they form a number of features. They normally start with the sea wearing away at a weakness, such as a fault in the rock. As more and more material is eroded *sea caves* gradually form. As sea caves meet, they form *arches*. Eventually, the gap gets so wide the overlying rock falls into the sea, leaving a *stack*. This in turn is eroded, and leaves a *stump* a little way out to sea as the coastline recedes still further (see Figure 19, showing Durdle Door in Dorset).

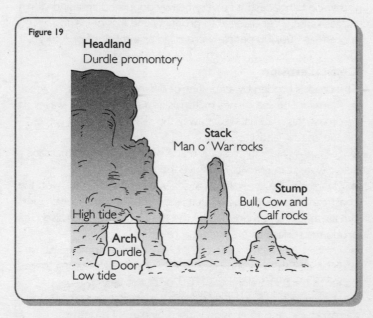

Figure 19

Headland
Durdle promontory

Stack
Man o´ War rocks

Stump
Bull, Cow and
Calf rocks

High tide

Arch
Durdle
Door

Low tide

Figure 20

Open coast. Reasonably straight coast with no visible headlands – for example, Pevensey.

Pevensey

Headland. Piece of coast that sticks out into the sea – for example, Land's End.

Land's End

Embayment. Broad curving bay with either a narrow or wide opening – for example, Pagham Harbour.

Pagham Harbour

Spit. Narrow stretch of coastline that curves out into the sea and is made of sand or shingle – for example, Spurn Head.

Spurn Head

Tombolo. Similar to a spit, but joins an island with the shore – for example, Chesil Beach.

Chesil Beach

Strait. Narrow stretch of water between two areas of land – for example, The Solent.

The Solent

Estuary. Where the sea occupies part of a river valley when the tide rises – for example, the estuary of the River Dee.

River Dee

Ria. Drowned river valley, much deeper than an estuary – for example, Salcombe.

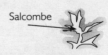
Salcombe

Bar. Long ridge of beach material, just out to sea, which runs parallel to the coast – for example, Scolt Head Island.

Scolt Head Island

So far, we have tended to concentrate on high cliff environments. However, much of our coast is backed by *sand dunes*. They are a fascinating environment to study with children as an introduction to ecosystems.

Sand dunes form in places with strong onshore winds, a good supply of sand and a wide tidal range. These let the sand dry out and get blown towards land. It gets trapped by vegetation and other objects. It gradually builds up and marram grass and sea couch start to colonise. As the dune is built up towards the sea, species such as heather and gorse start to colonise further inland where the wind is lighter. Rotting vegetation starts to build up a soil structure.

Rocky shores are also very interesting places for children to study. Most children enjoy exploring rock pools. They are an excellent introduction to ecosystems and provide opportunities for children to carefully observe and record. They can then offer explanations for what they have found.

A huge range of living things exist in areas of rocky shores. Some only exist below low-tide level, such as spider crabs and sea urchins. Others live in parts flooded at high tide, such as barnacles and sea horses. These environments demonstrate the importance of light, temperature, humidity and the effect of waves (see Figure 21).

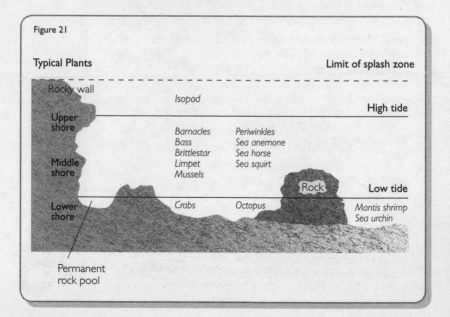

Figure 21

Sea level

Changes in sea level are of growing interest. Suggestions are being made that global warming is having a growing effect on our planet. It's a little more complex than is sometimes suggested in the media. Relative sea and land level changes have occurred since the formation of the Earth. For instance, sea levels all round the Earth rose at the end of the last ice age as the ice melted. These are called *eustatic changes*. Also, when parts of the Earth were covered in ice sheets, the land beneath them sagged down. As the ice receded, this land gradually moved up with the release in ice pressure. This has resulted in a relative fall in sea level. These adjustments are still happening around the world today and are called *isostatic changes*.

However, in some places we can see examples of *drowned coasts* or areas of *submergence*. This occurred where coastlines were drowned by sea level rises caused by ice melting. The Fowey estuary in Cornwall is one example, as is a *ria*. The estuary area was not glaciated and is therefore not moving through isostatic changes.

However, where coastlines were covered in ice, *raised coasts*, or areas of *emergence*, occur. Northern England and parts of Scotland have raised beaches that show how landscapes moved up once the weight of ice was removed.

To make the situation even more interesting, there is evidence that some parts of the south-east of England are subsiding. The Domesday Book lists many villages that are now under the North Sea.

Estimates have been made about the effect of global warming on sea levels. Environment Agency figures predict an annual rise in global mean sea level of 4mm per year over the 21st century. In places where the land is subsiding, this will be greater. Where land is emerging, the effect will be less. The Thames estuary comes within the area of subsidence and this is one reason for the building of the Thames Barrier, completed in 1982.

Why you need to know these facts

Coastal areas provide an excellent resource for geographical enquiries. With this knowledge, you can interpret what you observe on the coast and support children in their learning.

Vocabulary

Abrasion – the wearing away of a river bed and bank by its load.
Backwash – the movement of water down a beach.
Groyne – wooden or concrete walls built out into the sea to help prevent a beach being eroded by longshore drift.
Longshore drift – the gradual movement of particles along a beach as they are carried by the swash and backwash.
Swash – the movement of water up a beach.
Tombolo – a ridge of sand and shingle linking an island to the mainland.

Amazing facts

Tides can be very powerful: they are estimated to be able to move 70 million tons of sand in the Mersey estuary every 20 years.

Common misconceptions

The sea only erodes the land mass.
In fact, it often moves the materials it has eroded and deposits them at other points along the coast. The Lincolnshire coast is an interesting example of this.

Questions

Where does the sea get the energy to erode the coast?
It comes from two sources: ocean water masses are pushed and pulled by the gravitational force of the Moon, which causes the tides; and winds out to sea set sea water in motion and these forces are transferred towards the coast.

Handy tip

● Use a sand-tray river model (see Figure 17 on page 144). Put paper flags on wooden lolly sticks and write a key river word on each flag, such as *valley, estuary, stream, meander, delta*. Occasionally, turn off the water and ask children to put the flags where the features are. This can be a useful assessment activity.

● Collect a wide range of clear and detailed colour photographs of rivers and coasts from around the world. Books of aerial photographs from discount bookshops, old calendars and travel brochures are a few sources to search. These can be used to extend children's experience and knowledge in practical activities and classroom displays.

Teaching ideas

Modelling the effect of rain

Models are easy to make and can simulate the real world effectively. At KS1, they provide children with structured water and sand play. Ask children to make a model island in the sand tray. Then get them to make it rain on the island by using a small watering can. Ask them to watch what happens to the water. Then get them to put small model homes on the island where they think they won't be washed away in the next storm.

Modelling waves on the coast

Many river and coastal processes take thousands of years. Models can speed them up. Ask the children to push all the sand up into one half of the tray to make a coast with cliffs and bays. Push it together really firmly. Very gently, pour some water in to make the sea. Then use a plastic ruler to gently make waves. Ask the children to watch what happens to their coast. Do different things happen in different places? Why is this?

Human effects on the coast

Subject facts

People affect coastal areas in many ways. Some are very obvious, like the construction of an oil refinery. Others, such as walkers gradually eroding parts of a sand dune, are much less obvious, but can have considerable long-term effects. When you study coastlines with children, it is important to help them begin to understand the relationships between natural and human processes. This section provides the facts on how humans affect coastlines.

Fishing

A major global concern at the present time is over-fishing of the planet's stock of fish. It is a clear example of unsustainable activity. If we were able to fish at a rate that allowed stocks to be maintained (and perhaps even grow) through natural processes, we would be fishing in a sustainable way. However, this is not the case at either a national or a global scale. Many fishing techniques are not selective. This results in some species being killed but not used. Recent concerns over dolphin-friendly tuna fishing are an example of this and one to which children readily relate. If some fish species are removed from their ecosystem this can have further effects up and down the food chain. Some habitat damage can also result and this is an area for much further research.

The building of fishing ports and fish processing industries also affects our coastlines. Waste products from fish processing are often thrown back into the sea and can alter habitats by encouraging new species into an area. Lost fishing gear can wash ashore and affect wildlife along our coasts.

Coastal fish farms produce large amounts of effluent that is often disposed of in the sea, causing local habitat changes and pollution.

Urbanisation

Building towns and cities on coastlines changes them dramatically. The loss of visual amenities is quite obvious but more processes than just this take place. Natural coastal habitats are lost to buildings, which in turn can reduce species diversity. Water pollution from built-up areas often reaches the sea nearby. A major example of this is the dumping of raw sewage out to sea through pipelines. Where these built-up areas include port facilities, dredging to keep the port open can alter the ecosystems and wildlife habitats.

Tidal **barrages** also affect coastlines. The Tees barrage and Thames barrage are two examples. They change the amount, temperature and content of water reaching the sea. This can result in sediments building up behind the barrages and changing local ecosystems. Dams upstream of rivers can also change coastal environments by, for example, preventing the fine sediments needed by some organisms from reaching the sea.

Industry

Industry is located in coastal areas for many reasons. Some factories use materials that are imported and others produce goods that are exported. Coastal locations help to keep down transport costs. However, this can result in pollution when industries dispose of waste products into the sea. For instance, during the period of intensive coal mining in County Durham, much waste material from the coal industry was dumped at the coast. As a result, huge reclamation schemes were aimed at returning the area to a more natural and less polluted habitat. While the surface landscape has been improved, when the mines closed the pumping out of water was also stopped. This has since led to a build-up of water in the mines which is now finding its way to the surface. Unfortunately, this water contains many chemicals collected on its route through the disused mines, thus it is polluted.

If sea water is extracted for industrial processes, it can be returned to the sea either at a higher temperature or containing pollutants. Coastal power stations that use river water often pump cooling water into the sea at high temperatures. This affects the coastal environment.

Agriculture

Where land is reclaimed to increase agricultural use, coastal areas on each side of the scheme can be affected. This has occurred in areas around the Wash and now landowners are encouraged to return land to the sea in order to preserve long stretches of coast. We are gradually learning about the knock-on effects of such reclamation.

Fertilisers and pesticides used in coastal areas often find their way into coastal waters. These affect natural ecosystems through a process called eutrophication. This happens when nutrient-rich water reaches bodies of unpolluted water. Algae blooms and other species decline through oxygen starvation. Research is still taking place into the actual effects of nitrogen fertilisers reaching the sea through water courses and the deposition of phosphates into the sea from farm sewage. The Biotechnology and Biological Sciences Research Council (BBSRC) together with the National Science Foundation (NSF) is developing an 'Ideas Lab', aimed at finding new ways of growing crops without relying heavily on nitrogen fertilisers. This is an increasingly important issue because globally we have got to produce much more food, but using less fertiliser in order to reduce pollution.

If fresh water is extracted from rivers on their way to the sea, this changes the balance of fresh water mingling with salt water in coastal areas. Again, this can change the balance of living things in coastal areas.

Tourism and recreation

Globally, tourism is growing rapidly. Coastlines are built up to accommodate hotels and entertainments. Water run-off is changed and can cause localised erosion. Sea water is extracted for human uses which don't need fresh water. Waste water and sewage is pumped into the sea. In some places, where rapid development is taking place with few controls, the intensity of pollution can be high. The construction of ports and marinas changes the natural shape of the coastline. We are beginning to learn that this can have serious consequences along the coast on either side of such developments, for both biological and physical processes.

Noise and disturbance to the water can deter some native species, which in turn affects the local **ecology** of an area. Much tourist development in coastal areas takes place because of the natural beauty of the area before development. Quite often, human communities have lived in these places for generations, living in sustainable ways. Large-scale tourist development can affect the native human population in positive and negative ways. It can bring new and higher-paid employment, but people can lose their independence. Local skills and traditions can be lost or turned into tourist attractions. Sometimes, as is happening in parts of the Mediterranean developed during the 1960s, developments are seen as out-of-date and lacking in facilities. This leads to a decline in their popularity and a form of coastal urban decay begins to occur. New development sites are sought thus placing even greater pressure on a decreasing supply of natural coastal areas.

Why you need to know these facts

Many children will have some first-hand experience of streams, rivers or coastal areas. But these places are full of quite complex and inter-related processes. Primary teachers need to understand how the various parts work and fit together. This will provide you with the confidence to help children to develop enquiries in these areas.

Vocabulary

Deposition – takes place when a river drops its load of sand, pebbles, vegetation and other materials.
Erosion – removal of rock, soil and plant materials by a river.
Eutrophication – a process in bodies of water where too many nutrients encourage algae blooms, cause oxygen starvation and result in fewer species being present.
Gradient – the angle at which a river flows downhill through the landscape.
Spit – a place where deposits of sand and shingle extend a beach into the sea.
Transportation – carrying of materials (load) by a river.
Velocity – the speed of water in a river.

Amazing facts

It is estimated that parts of the Suffolk coastline have moved inland by 3km since Roman times due to coastal erosion. All evidence of human activity has been lost or buried beneath the North Sea.

Common misconceptions

Coastal areas are linked purely to holiday and leisure.
Children often visit the coast for holiday and other leisure activities. It's crucial that they understand that coastal areas are important for other activities, such as ports and industrial sites.

Teaching ideas

Visit the coast
It's not easy to recreate coastal areas in the classroom. Even today, with increased mobility, some children rarely visit the coast. As a whole school, look at your geography schemes of work to see where visits to the coast may be placed. The physical experience of watching waves, hearing the noises of the sea and exploring beaches will help to teach children many of the ideas covered in this chapter. Health and safety requirements are essential and are covered in Chapter 6 (see pages 168–169).

Link with a coastal school
If it is impossible to arrange a visit to the coast, consider choosing a coastal locality to study within your scheme. Link up with a school on the coast: they will be able to provide artefacts such as sand and rock samples, tourist leaflets, maps, aerial photographs, videos and children's accounts of what the coast is like and how it is changing.

Resources

A wide range of constantly changing features can be found on coastlines. Although we have satellite images and maps, they don't show everything. Project Neptune has been running since 1965 and works with many organisations, including the National Trust, to protect Britain's coastline. Visit the website to learn more about the project, its past and upcoming appeals, and to view a plethora of coastal images: **www.neptunecoastlinecampaign.org.uk**

Useful reading

How We Use and Abuse Our Planet: Water by Grant, P. & Haswell, A. (London: Chrysalis Books, 2004).

'Rivers, coasts and the landscape' by Lewis, L., in *Primary Geography Handbook* edited by Scoffham, S. (Sheffield: Geographical Association, 2010).

Hot Topics: Weather and Climate by Peter Riley (Scholastic Ltd, 2012).

Teaching resources

CD-ROMs – KS2

The Earth and Its Geography (ZigZag Multimedia)

Rivers (Ransom Publishing)

Websites

Miami Museum of Science Ecolinks – Hydrosphere:
www.miamisci.org/ecolinks/hydrosphere.html

Water Aid:
www.wateraid.org/Water

KS2 activity links:
www.strettonhandley.derbyshire.sch.uk/waterlinks.html

The water cycle explained:
www.topicbox.net/geography/geography_water_cycle

Chapter 6

Fieldwork

This chapter looks at fieldwork with regards to the types
of fieldwork you should carry out with your class, as well as
covering how to plan fieldwork, health and safety, and how
to incorporate ICT into your lessons, which will all provide a
framework for developing effective fieldwork in the 21st century.

Why do fieldwork?

Subject facts

Fieldwork takes children's learning out into the real world
and provides them with first-hand experiences. They visit new
places and meet new people. Children do see many places
around the world through television and digital media, but
this is all second-hand experience. Fieldwork helps children
to understand that these experiences do not give them the
full picture: it helps them to develop critical skills in citizenship
and understanding and valuing other people and places. For
example, it is possible to watch a video about how coastlines are
changing but it is a much more vivid experience to visit a beach,
see the waves moving, feel the pressure of the water, hear the
noises of the waves and the birds, and smell the scents of the
seaside. While some families can give children these experiences,
there are many children who only experience them through
school activities.

Fieldwork gives children a context for asking geographical
questions and devising enquiries. It makes these meaningful
because they are working with real places, people, events,
objects and questions.

Well-planned fieldwork helps children to develop their curiosity about the real world. It can help them to become interested in the world around them by giving them the skills to look carefully and ask questions about what they see, hear, touch and smell.

Fieldwork can challenge children. For some KS1 children, it might be learning to go for a walk together in a local park and share a picnic. For some inner-city KS2 children, it could be the achievement of walking across open countryside following the course of a river. Good planning can build in many aspects of personal and social education.

Real-world experiences are important at the foundation stage, and fieldwork is a critical part of any geography curriculum at KS1 and KS2.

Why you need to know these facts

Good fieldwork takes time, but geography is often only given limited time in the school curriculum. Fieldwork needs very careful planning to ensure the inclusion of valuable learning experiences and proper safety. This takes up staff time that already has many demands on it. It can also have a cost factor for both parents and the school. People will want to know precisely why the fieldwork is needed and what children will learn.

Vocabulary

Fieldwork – studying the world, going beyond the classroom.
Inclusion – the need to ensure all children have appropriate access to fieldwork experiences.
Risk assessment – the regular checking of fieldwork locations to assess their dangers and potential.

Handy tip

- Success tends to build on success! Once you have established a relevant, effective and enjoyable fieldwork programme, it will become a highly valued part of school life. This chapter contains the information you need to make fieldwork successful.

● You can ask parents to make voluntary contributions for visits beyond school, but many families find it hard to make these payments or cannot see the value of such visits. If your whole-school fieldwork policy includes the reasons why fieldwork is an integral part of the curriculum and shows how it relates to relevant subjects, you may find it easier to get parental support.

Types of fieldwork

Subject facts

Where?
Fieldwork experiences can happen in different places. To illustrate this more fully, let's look at water as a focus for fieldwork:

> **Water**
> **The school building and grounds**. What happens to rainwater around the school?
> **The locality surrounding the school**. Visit a local stream.
> **The region beyond the school**. In a coach, follow part of the course of a river in the region, stopping at key places.
> **A distant place in the UK**. Compare a faraway stream or river with the local stream or river while on a residential field visit.
> **A distant place overseas**. For some schools, this may happen during a residential visit in another country, when studying a river there.

Realistically, not all schools can do this. However, there is the idea of virtual fieldwork as an alternative. We'll look at this later in the chapter (see pages 177–182).

Fieldwork can provide different experiences in familiar and unfamiliar surroundings. Children may think they know their locality because they are in it every day. Carefully planned investigations can help them to see new things and ask questions about things they take for granted. This is also a skill many adults find interesting. Visiting unfamiliar surroundings might also involve meeting new people who they do not normally see in their familiar places, for example a forest ranger whom they would not normally have an opportunity to meet in their city.

For whom?

Fieldwork can be planned for different types of group. You can plan to take the whole class out or it may be more appropriate to arrange for smaller groups to complete the fieldwork. These may all be doing the same thing or each group can have a different task that will contribute towards a whole-class jigsaw activity. Individuals can do fieldwork. Schools normally support this through homework or activities for individual children to do on holiday.

When?

Fieldwork can be planned for different periods of time. Children can go out for small periods of time, such as when collecting weather data in parts of the school grounds. Sometimes a half-day trip based on a short walk from the school can be time- and cost-effective as no expensive transport is needed. Well-planned whole-day trips may be more appropriate for some fieldwork activities. Residential visits lasting a few days can be an integral part of effective fieldwork programmes.

By whom?

Fieldwork activities can be planned so that children and teachers have different roles. The Geographical Association's Field Studies Working Group has developed a model to explain the possibilities. See their website: **www.geography.org.uk/resources/fieldwork**

● *Teacher as director or instructor.* Here, you or another adult tells children things about the place they are visiting. You control the activities and what children do. This role is useful when you wish to have full control over children to help them learn some new skills or look at something in detail. It might mean giving them information, for example showing them different types of home and using the correct vocabulary. It could be to help children to begin to ask questions about a place by perhaps talking to a local person, modelling the questioning method. In the teacher-as-director model, the children receive facts and ideas from adults; they may respond to questions; they follow given instructions. Children work within a prescribed framework with defined outcomes. For example, you ask children to select two buildings in a street and draw them. They must label the parts and look for clues to show what they are used for. Clear objectives of observation, field sketching and problem-solving are present, but opportunities for pupil-directed enquiry are small. There are times when this role is effective and good fieldwork planning will identify when to use it.

● *Teacher as facilitator.* Here, you or another adult acts as a guide to help children with their learning. You provide an environment in which children identify questions and issues for an enquiry in the field. For example, if you are working in a local street, you ask children to focus on land use, but it is their job to work out what they will study and how they will collect relevant information. This type of fieldwork enables children to take responsibility for the planning and implementation of their investigations. This can create different roles for children. Instead of being receivers of information, they use skills to answer questions and solve problems. In this situation, teachers and other adults pose questions, encourage children to use different skills and ensure their decisions keep them on the enquiry task. The framework may adapt as children carry out their research and unplanned outcomes may occur. Children may decide they wish to do something as a result of what they have found out, for example that more trees and shrubs are needed in the school grounds to bring in more wildlife, and write to a local garden centre asking if they might donate some to the school.

When planning fieldwork, you need to consider when these various roles for children and teachers are most appropriate and how long they should last. Naturally, whatever role you take, health and safety issues must always be kept firmly in mind.

Why you need to know these facts

It's hard to fit geography fieldwork into a busy primary curriculum. Therefore, it is important to choose the most effective way of organising your various fieldwork activities.

Knowing why you have selected a particular method will also help you to justify the work to parents, governors and other interested people. Incidentally, Ofsted inspectors would like to observe more fieldwork during inspections. Many schools avoid this when in fact it is an excellent opportunity to demonstrate effective geography teaching.

Vocabulary

Fieldwork programme – a whole-school plan that provides progress and continuity of children's fieldwork experiences.
Teacher as instructor – a model of teaching in which knowledge and ideas are transferred from the teacher to children.
Teacher as facilitator – a model of teaching where teachers provide a rich environment that helps the children to become independent learners.

Common misconceptions

You have to plan fieldwork in more distant places for older children only.
A well-planned visit beyond the locality can be an excellent learning experience for younger children.

Handy tip

In Chapter 3, we discussed how places can be connected and how much of geography is the study of patterns and processes. Fieldwork is an excellent time to help children to understand and learn this. For instance, by seeing how a river flows through unpolluted places before it reaches their town, children can begin to understand how what happens in one place can affect somewhere else. They could then look at the course of the river after it leaves the town for signs of pollution that may not have been present upstream.

Your fieldwork programme

Subject facts

Subject leaders are responsible for whole-school policies for their subject. However, when you're planning fieldwork for your class you do need to know what the children have learned before and what they will be taught further up the school. You need to be aware of the whole-school geography scheme of work. Fieldwork can be a very successful way of building on previous learning, but you need to know what new knowledge, skills and understanding will be developed by what you plan.

As well as planning what your objectives are in order to meet the children's learning requirements, it is also important to ensure that your objectives are realistic within the time and resources available. Think about the needs of all children to ensure that they have equal opportunities.

Having considered these points, you need to move on to plan fieldwork that will include all or some of the following:

● *Opportunities to develop geographical enquiries.* These may have begun in the classroom.

● *Time to learn new skills and practise those already experienced.* For instance, children may have made simple plans with their own key and you now want them to use maps with more abstract symbols in the key.

● *Activities to gain new geographical knowledge.* Children may have a basic vocabulary for describing buildings and land, but by planning a simple land use survey, they will be able to extend this.

● *Experiences in which social skills and citizenship activities can be developed.* For example, when interviewing local people about an issue, children learn that different people have different points of view.

Try to plan a range of fieldwork experiences. Look for cross-curricular links to support other work across subject areas. For example, if you are studying the Tudors at some point in the year, see if there are any Tudor buildings where you are going and incorporate this into the trip.

If you decide to return to a fieldwork site, you need to know that revisiting it is going to be relevant to previous learning. You also need to be sure that learning will be furthered.

Parents

Some schools have a clear fieldwork policy, which explains to parents why the fieldwork is important. If parents understand the importance of fieldwork and are given plenty of notice, they may be more supportive and understanding.

Parents may need time to budget for the costs of fieldwork. Make public what you will be doing. It's surprising how often people will then offer help in terms of information, objects, visits or access to places of interest.

If you have help from parents or other adults on field visits, it's worth briefing them on the specific geographical aims you have. For example, at KS1, you may want children to learn geographical vocabulary or make simple drawings. At KS2, children may need to be shown how to use simple surveying equipment to draw a map. Parents need guidance in how to help achieve these aims.

The Geographical Association's Field Studies Working Group offers this summary of quality planning for fieldwork, to create a purposeful, enjoyable experience through which learning becomes fun:

● Careful and imaginative planning.
● Thorough preparation, including exploratory pre-visit, briefing all participants, and use of appropriate, sufficient and well-maintained equipment.
● Responsible conduct of the fieldwork.
● Productive follow-up of the experience.
● Thorough post-fieldwork review.

Why you need to know these facts

Good planning helps you and your children to get the most out of fieldwork. The more confident you are, the more you will probably enjoy the work because the children will sense your interest and composure.

Teaching ideas

Design activities that make children look closely at the fieldwork environment and ask questions. For example, provide each child with a photograph that they have to match to its location and mark on a map during the visit. Write an open-ended question on the back, for example *Why are no houses built near the river?*

Fieldwork health and safety and risk assessment

Subject facts

It is essential that you have visited beforehand the area where the fieldwork will take place. When you are there you need to do two things. The first is the detailed planning of the learning experiences. This will identify what is there, where you will go and what will take place. We will look at these more closely in the two case studies later in this chapter. The second is to carry out a risk analysis.

Risk assessment

This list – from Richardson in the *Primary Geography Handbook*, edited by Scoffham, S. (Sheffield: Geographical Association, 2010) – gives essential points to cover when assessing a site for risk:

1. Identify the hazards that could occur at the location.
2. Decide on what could happen as a result of the hazard and who might be affected.
3. Evaluate the risks involved and decide whether or not the precautions taken are sufficient or whether more are needed.
4. Record and date your findings, and find out whether or not there will be any significant changes before your visit.
5. Review the risk assessment before a further visit is made.

The following examples taken from actual visits illustrate these points in practice:

● A footpath beside a river may be safe when you do the risk assessment but will it still be safe if there's heavy rain the day before your visit?

● During a KS1 visit to a farm, the farmer will show children some baby animals. Will they touch them? Are there facilities for washing their hands after this experience?

● At KS2, a survey is planned in a shopping street. How busy will it be at the time when the children are there? Will they be able to stand in places safe from traffic?

The Department for Education and Skills' *Learning Outside the Classroom MANIFESTO* (Nottingham: DfES Publications, 2006) provides further information on how to carry out a risk assessment exercise.

Why you need to know these facts

It is important to record your risk assessment and give your headteacher a copy to file. If a site is used regularly, the risk assessment will need to be updated because no place stays the same. For example, a once-empty field which you cross via a footpath may have cows in it on a future visit. The school needs to show that it has a clear policy and system for monitoring activities in the wider world. If something does go wrong, it can then demonstrate that everything possible was done to prevent, or at least minimise, problems.

Fieldwork must never be dangerous or too risky to attempt. Media reports of accidents that take place on field visits or at outdoor residential centres have a negative effect on teachers' willingness to plan such activities, as well as parents' willingness to give support. You will always be acting *in loco parentis*. No activity in the real world is without risk, whether organised by teachers or parents. You must do all you can to minimise the risks connected with the activity.

We all have the best interests of children at the front of our minds: safe and enjoyable fieldwork may help them to develop a lifelong interest in the wider world.

Vocabulary

Accountability – as teachers, we are responsible for the welfare of our children while they are in our care.

In loco parentis – teachers are expected in law to maintain the levels of safety that could be expected of a reasonable parent.

Handy tip

If the school does not already have something similar, suggest that a simple field visit sheet is designed for school use. It might contain the following headings:

- Place of field visit.
- Contact person.
- Address and phone/email.
- Date last visited.
- Learning activities offered.
- Curriculum links for activities.
- Age/ability range suitability.
- Facilities: educational, domestic and for special needs.
- Equipment to be taken.
- Positive features.
- Negative features.
- Changes taking place.

A risk assessment sheet could be clipped to this and then placed in an easily accessible file. This is a practical way in which the school can demonstrate that it takes the organisation and monitoring of fieldwork seriously.

Planning fieldwork

This section contains ideas for fieldwork in the Foundation stage, KS1 and KS2. They provide you with the information to be considered when planning relevant, interesting and safe fieldwork. The ideas are on the theme of food and cultures from around the world to demonstrate how progress and continuity may be achieved in geographical learning.

Subject facts

Foundation stage – four- and five-year-olds

The foundations of knowledge and understanding of the world are laid in these years. Experiences should be planned for children both in and beyond the school. They could taste fruits from different parts of the world and be shown the countries on a big inflatable globe. They could be asked to think how the fruit might have reached them. People from **ethnic groups** in the community could be invited in to make simple dishes with them. They could listen to music from other countries and learn simple dances. They could visit an Indian restaurant and see the similarities and differences between that kitchen and the one at home. They might watch a video of life in an Indian village.

Why you need to know these facts

Children at this stage need opportunities to see objects, people and images from around the world. This will encourage them to begin to think about other people and places. It introduces similarities and differences. It provides a foundation for citizenship education and PSHE by fostering a respect for other values, cultures and ways of life. It helps children to start asking questions. They will start to learn that places are connected to each other.

If some of the learning experiences can be provided by parents, they will be integrated more fully into the learning process and the life of the school. This can help parents to feel that they provide a valuable and valued part of their children's education.

Subject facts

KS1 fieldwork case study

The theme of food and cultures in the community can be extended at KS1. The fieldwork activities described below will develop children's knowledge and understanding of places.

Fieldwork

Using a simple plan, children can walk around the local shopping area with adults. They can find shops, restaurants and cultural facilities, such as mosques, that represent people and places from other countries. They can use a simple key to mark them on their maps.

A visit can be arranged to one or more places. Children can plan a simple geographical enquiry by deciding beforehand things they want to know. They can use ICT in the form of digital cameras and voice recorders to collect information.

They can find food, clothing and artefacts made from products from other countries during their fieldwork. For example, a Chinese restaurant may have some interesting prints of Chinese views on a calendar. These could show children much about the landscape, buildings and climate of other places.

By visiting buildings of religious importance, children will begin to understand and respect beliefs, values and traditions from other places. The links between geography, RE and citizenship are rarely made full use of in school planning processes and such visits provide an excellent opportunity. Children can see different styles of architecture and decoration. They can listen to music from distant places and hear people talk in other languages, perhaps even learning some simple words.

Artefacts from the local community can teach children many things about other places. For example, a wood-burning tandoor oven in an Indian restaurant can be a starting point for investigating how local resources influence the ways in which things are designed and built. It could also introduce issues of sustainable development by looking at how the design of the oven allows it to make full use of the fuel used.

Back at school, children can build a simple model of the shopping area, with links to other places clearly marked. A world map can be fixed behind the model and wool used to link each building with the appropriate country.

Fieldwork can be extended by using ICT. Children might search the internet to link with a primary school in India. They can produce simple reports of their enquiries using their digital photos in a simple desktop publishing package and these could be added to their model of the shopping area. Finally, some examples of products and artefacts from other places can be added to the display to help children to understand where various things come from.

Why you need to know these facts

These practical examples show how everyday parts of a
school locality can be used to achieve clear geographical
learning through active fieldwork. All school localities are unique;
the purpose of the examples is to encourage you to look
carefully at your own locality for the opportunities it provides for
relevant and interesting fieldwork.

Vocabulary

Progression in fieldwork – the need to ensure that each
fieldwork experience builds upon previous work and extends
children's experience and understanding.

Common misconceptions

*Extensive worksheets are not really a very effective
tool for active geographical enquiry.*
The examples provided show how children can learn about
other places and the links between them by looking carefully
in a structured environment, asking questions and choosing
effective ways to record their findings. The display reinforces
the many things learned, makes use of geographical resources
such as a world map and begins to show how places can
be linked.

Handy tip

Do all you can to find out what your locality has to offer.
Make contacts with local people and show how they can
become a valued part of the school community.

Fieldwork

Subject facts

KS2 fieldwork case study

The theme can be further extended by fieldwork at KS2 by visiting your town or city centre, or one in a larger place further afield. For example, if your school is in Wetherby, it would be practical to plan a day's visit to Sheffield city centre.

Such planning provides children with the opportunity to study at a larger range of scales in new environments. They will learn more complex geographical skills. For example, they can follow the route there on a smaller-scale regional map. While doing fieldwork in the city centre, they will use more complex orienteering skills with detailed plans of the area. There will be many new experiences that can extend their geographical vocabulary. For instance, the public transport system in Sheffield is organised in an attempt to address demands on the environment while meeting the needs of a large population.

On the journey there, the children will travel down the A1 and see a number of electricity power stations. They can note what they see and develop further research back at school. For example, what fuel is used to generate electricity in the power stations? Where is the source of the River Aire and what counties does it flow through? Where does it reach the sea?

Once in Sheffield, you can arrange for children to travel into the centre by the new tram system. Before the visit, children can plan where to ask the coach driver to take them in order to reach the correct tram station. What direction will they be travelling in? Some children can use compasses to find the answer.

On arrival in the city centre, children will have to find their position on a plan by identifying key landmarks and orientating the plan. Such fieldwork at KS2 is an excellent opportunity to plan jigsaw enquiries. The class is divided into perhaps six groups, each with an enquiry task that they designed back at school. Excellent adult supervision is essential. Helpers will need clear advice on the geographical learning that can be achieved through careful questioning and the development of observational skills. Your risk assessment will have included the dangers of traffic and being able to find safe places to interview shoppers, for example.

Back at school, children can prepare presentations on their group enquiries, and speaking and listening skills within the literacy requirements may be met in a meaningful and stimulating way.

One group can visit a religious building of a faith not yet covered by earlier fieldwork. They can use previously developed enquiry skills to look more closely and ask more detailed questions of those people showing them around. When they make their presentation, they can compare their findings with those from the earlier local visit.

Another two groups might be responsible for completing a land use survey of a carefully chosen part of the city centre. This will have been chosen by you to include a wide range of buildings and features representing an even greater variety of countries than available in your locality. Back at school, the children's map can be related to a world map showing the location of the countries represented and perhaps some patterns may be seen. An example would be the concentration of Chinese restaurants in one or two streets. Children can then be asked to suggest reasons why this geographical pattern has developed. They can offer possible solutions in their presentation.

This group could offer personal views on the quality of the environment in various places. This could focus on traffic fumes, noise, interesting buildings or litter. Children could say what they like and dislike, offering reasons for their choices. They could compare their observations with what they see in their own locality. Such activities build environmental change and sustainable development into the fieldwork in a practical way.

Another group can question shoppers in various locations. They might focus on which shops they use that have connections with other countries and why they use them. Alternatively, they could ask where people have come from, the transport they used and the main reason they have come to Sheffield. Back at school, the results can be plotted on maps and data analysed through ICT packages. Some interesting patterns may be seen and this group can offer ideas to explain them.

Another group might visit a community centre that represents a particular culture. Their task will be to find out about the ways of life in the community, the concerns and hopes of the people, their values and beliefs. They could learn to sing a song that one of the group could record to play in their presentation. They can

Fieldwork

find out about the meaning of the song, thus broadening their understanding of other cultures.

The final group could visit an urban school where a wide range of cultural backgrounds is represented. They might be paired with individual children and experience a part of their school day, with lunch being an excellent time to consider different foods and perhaps religious values. They can have questions prepared about what the children do in their own time, where they play and what they play. This will probably produce a large number of similarities as well as some interesting differences. They can compare the school with their own, and learn important social skills in respecting other environments and learning to be sensitive and responsible visitors. Back at school, this group might plan a role-play that shows a day in the life of some of the children they have met. With many schools having websites and email links, such enquiries could continue after the actual fieldwork has taken place.

Working in groups like this can help to ensure that appropriate and differentiated geographical activities are experienced by all children. If adult helpers are well briefed about the aims and objectives for their groups, they can support children in maintaining a geographical focus.

Why you need to know these facts

These examples show how skills and knowledge from the foundation stage and KS1 have been carefully extended into more demanding activities for older children. Such a field visit will be costly in teacher planning time and there will be financial costs to parents. You will need to be able to justify all the activities and explain how they develop children's knowledge and understanding.

Vocabulary

Jigsaw activity – the use of a selection of geographical enquiries that build up into a larger project.

Other UK locality – an area that can easily and safely be studied during a day visit. It should be of similar size to the locality of your school.

Handy tip

● All the group activities do need careful planning, with particular attention paid to learning outcomes and safety issues. However, teachers who have conducted such fieldwork find that the effort required is more than made up for in the high quality of pupil learning and motivation created by being in a new and challenging environment.

● Also, the examples demonstrate how careful planning allows such geographically based activities to reinforce and complement other areas of the school curriculum such as literacy, ICT and citizenship. It provides real-world experiences to which to apply cross-curricular skills and knowledge.

Virtual fieldwork

Subject facts

Real-world experiences of people, places and events, both close to school and further afield, enrich children's understanding of the world. However, it's not possible to physically travel to all parts of the world from primary school! The availability of ever-developing information and communication technology can provide ways of extending children's experience of the world.

The following examples demonstrate how different types of technology may be used to support their learning about the world through what is called 'virtual fieldwork'. However, it must be said that virtual fieldwork should not be seen as an alternative to first-hand experience of out-of-classroom activities, but as another set of tools to be employed when, for whatever reason, it may not be possible to visit the places to carry out enquiry. It may also be worth seeing the tools of virtual fieldwork in two ways:

● The first is the more obvious one of giving children access to people, places and events they may not otherwise experience. The benefits of this are that these experiences are current and not taken from some out-of-date printed source or DVD, for example.

● The second way of seeing virtual fieldwork tools is as a way of extending the recording of data collection from 'real fieldwork'. This then provides a wide range of information which the children can analyse in more depth back at school.

Email

Many pupils will be familiar with using email to communicate with friends and family. We therefore need to ask what geographical learning can take place via this medium. The skill here is to develop a cross-curricular approach with literacy. It is generally accepted in the world of geography education that there are five key questions to ask when studying a place and how people live within it. They are:

● Where is this place?
● What is this place like?
● Why is this place as it is?
● How is this place connected to other places?
● How is this place changing?

Some people like to add:

● How do you feel about this place?

This adds a further dimension of values, PSHE or citizenship into the geography curriculum.

Clearly, you will comply with the school IT policy on children working with emails during lessons. Once that is established, you then need to decide with whom the children will develop email communication. From my experience, this is best done by deciding on a locality either in Britain or further afield which has features that contrast with what the children experience in their own locality. This needs to be kept simple and also reliable to ensure that communication does not break down after a few messages. There are two points to consider here:

● The first is that a personal link with the teacher(s) working with the children you wish to link with generally ensures that people are committed to making the project work and last.

● The second is to ensure that your pupils know why they are making contact with other children via email. This is where you can plan real geographical enquiry and get your class to decide how they want to use the five or six geographical questions listed above to understand another place. Try to provide some photos, artefacts or some other resources as starting points. You can then look at whatever literacy curriculum requirements are currently in place and plan how those skills may be developed in different types of email communication. For example: asking questions, describing events, expressing how a place feels through poetry.

Video conferencing facilities

Children are increasingly familiar with this form of technology, often through their mobile phones. Once again, we need to ask why and how these can be effective tools for geographical enquiry. The same points discussed for emails in terms of developing geographical enquiry and making relevant links with other subjects still apply. The key difference is that the live, moving image adds another valuable dimension. You and your pupils need to know why they need this facility and what they want to use it for. There could be many objectives for this in your planning, such as the development of social skills for holding a discussion at a distance or preparing clear questions that children want to ask.

● Northwood Primary School's website has an example of using video conferencing to develop pupils' global understanding by basing their work on the 2012 Olympics. Arrange a video conference with them here: **www.northwood.org.uk**

The other geographical advantage is that the live conferencing can take place out in the field. Here are some examples of how it might look in practice:

● Pupils identify three different parts of their town. A group of pupils accompanied by an adult is sent to each part with their mobile device. They then study the area. When they are ready, they contact a pupil back in school to share what they have found. These findings can be downloaded and kept for further whole-class analysis. The class-based pupils can also suggest other questions that they could ask those children on location.

● Another effective use for video conferencing is on residential fieldwork. Perhaps at the end of each day parents can come into school and join a live webcam session with their children on the residential visit. This both gives a purpose for pupils' studies and helps to promote the benefits of fieldwork to parents and carers.

Digital cameras, video cameras and remote control/ movement sensor cameras

In one sense, these technologies are merging, with one device capable of performing a range of tasks. Their main advantage for geographical fieldwork is the flexibility with which the collected images can be used both in the field and for later follow-up. For example, one school has set up a movement sensor camera in the woodland on their school grounds. The children can study that environment during the day at first hand. By powering up their movement sensor camera to record activity during the night they can then watch and analyse the footage the following day. This has included the changing patterns of badger behaviour and use of territory at various times of the year. Digital cameras are now very light and simple to use. If you want aerial photos of your school locality, you could develop a design project to build a platform on which to support and raise a camera (think hot air balloons, polystyrene and string). Using the time delay on the camera you can take photos from the air and then use them straight away on laptops and interactive whiteboards in class.

Websites

With due regard to the school's policy on websites, they provide an increasingly valuable range of geographical resources. The issue for teachers is that they are not necessarily labelled 'geography', but they are! Here are some examples to get you started:

● maps.google.co.uk/help/maps/streetview – This is an excellent resource for you and your pupils to use to ask and answer geographical questions. For example, it can help children see how varied the world is. Divide your class up into six groups and give each a very different settlement to study. Their task could be to prepare a poster describing what it might be like to live in that place. Also, have a look at the Google® Pins facility. It offers a very easy way for children to place their findings onto a map of anywhere in the world and add comments and photographs.

● www.geograph.org.uk – This website contains photographs taken in almost every Ordnance Survey kilometre grid square covering the whole country. Many photos have information attached to them. It gives you and your pupils access to thousands of recent geographical images. You can also upload your own images to this carefully regulated site.

● www.worldmapper.org – This site contains hundreds of world maps showing a huge range of data sets including: doctors per 1000 people; deforestation levels; production numbers of cars. The clever part of the site is that the data is displayed so that the size of the country is equivalent to its contribution to the topic.

For example, proportionate to the actual size of the country, a country with a lot of doctors per 1000 people is displayed as much larger than countries with few doctors per 1000 people.

Many of the examples in this section are based on still and moving images. In this digital age, it is very easy for images to be wiped or become unaccessible. Do try your best to archive or print some of the images created during your real and virtual fieldwork activities, especially of your school locality. In years to come, future pupils and teachers will be pleased that you have left them resources that answer the key questions at the start of this section.

Why you need to know these facts

Technology is widely used in schools. However, it is not always apparent to busy teachers just how it may be used in various subject areas. These examples have been chosen to help you think about the possibilities there are in the facilities you currently have in school. You are required to plan the effective use of ICT into primary school subjects. Geography offers a wide range of ways in which to do this.

Common misconceptions

The technology is very complex.

This doesn't need to be the case. A carefully chosen set of colour prints taken in your locality can open up a wide range of interesting geographical work in the classroom. Where was the photograph taken? Who lives near there? What are people doing in the photo? How has the place changed?

Handy tip

If you use some of the technology described, you and your children will generate photographs, videos, CD-ROMs and other resources. While it's not always possible to keep everything, do think of those colleagues and children who will be in your school in five or ten years' time. They will be delighted if you keep some for them to study. You are creating a record of the present for the future. Children should understand the importance of labelling their resources, including dates and names of those involved, as well as the names of the places they show. We are all part of a constantly changing world. Your record of those changes will help future geographers understand the world in which they live.

Resources

Useful reading

Achieving QTS. Teaching Primary Geography by Catling, S. & Willy, T. (Exeter: Learning Matters, 2009).

Fieldwork File. For the Primary Years by May, S. & Richardson, P. (Sheffield: Geographical Association, 2006).

'The geography of happiness', *Primary Geographer*, Number 68 (Sheffield: Geographical Association, Spring 2009).

'Focus on graphicacy: Ways of looking at our world', *Primary Geography*, Number 75 (Sheffield: Geographical Association, Summer 2011).

'Fieldwork and outdoor learning' by Richardson, P., in *Primary Geography Handbook*, edited by Scoffham, S. (Sheffield: Geographical Association, 2010).

Thinking on the edge by Rowley, C. & Lewis, L. (London: Living Earth, 2003).

Other resources

Websites
www.field-studies-council.org
www.geography.org.uk/projects
www.google.co.uk/intl/en_uk/earth
maps.google.co.uk

Fieldwork equipment
This is a general list of useful equipment (the specific aims of a visit may need extra equipment, for example a river study will need wellingtons, measuring equipment, a water testing kit and so on): clipboards (A3 size makes sketching and writing easier);

plastic bags to keep work dry if it rains; selection of pencils and crayons; compass; binoculars for observing distant features; digital camera; digital audio recorder; stopwatch; simple soil-testing kit; large-scale plans of the area being studied; photographs; tape measures; cloud, tree and pond life identification charts; clinometers; plastic bags to collect samples, for example of soil; local leaflets and directories; quadrats; digital video camera for recording change, interviews and movement in the environment; mobile phone camera; GPS unit; iPad®.

Glossary

Agriculture – the use of land for growing crops and keeping animals.
Aid – the process of moving resources around the world to support people in need.
Air mass – a body of air that has similar temperatures and levels of humidity in it.
Atmosphere – the mixture of oxygen, nitrogen, carbon dioxide, argon and water vapour surrounding the Earth.
Axis – an imaginary line through the Earth connecting the north and south poles, around which the Earth moves.

Backwash – the movement of water down a beach.
Barrage – a structure built across a river to slow the flow of water and create a deeper water level.
Birth rate – the number of babies born each year per 1000 people in the population.

Canal – a waterway constructed by people.
Central Business District – the central part of a town or city, which contains major offices, large branches of banks, department stores, government offices and entertainment facilities.
Climate – average weather conditions for a particular place on Earth.
Community – traditionally, a group of people living close together and having similar needs and interests and support networks and services. Developments in information technology have now created communities of people who are linked across much greater distances.
Commuter – a person who travels from home to where they work.
Consumer – a person who uses goods (eg bread) and/or services (eg a bank).

Continent – the seven large areas of land on the Earth.

Conurbation – an area of built-up land created when once-separate settlements have grown and joined.

Crop – food (eg wheat) and non-food (eg oilseed rape) plants grown, for sale, in fields.

Dam – a barrier built across a river to build up the level of water behind it. This creates a reservoir of water for human use and hydroelectric power.

Demography – the study of populations to analyse how and why they change.

Deposition – the sand, pebbles and soil particles left behind by streams and rivers.

Desertification – the process of once-fertile land becoming a desert or semi-desert area. It is believed to be caused by increases in global population and climatic changes.

Dispersed settlement – a pattern of buildings thinly scattered across a landscape, eg isolated farms and cottages in remote areas.

Drought – a long period of time without rainfall or other precipitation, such as snow.

Ecology – the scientific study of the relationships between plant and animal organisms.

Economy – the system created by a society to create wealth through a range of activities and administrative ways.

Eco town – name given to a housing scheme which has an emphasis on affordable and sustainable living.

Equator – an imaginary line drawn around the middle of the Earth.

Erosion – the wearing away of the landscape by water, ice and wind.

Ethnic group – a group of people in a society who feel they have a distinct cultural identity.

Factory – a building where goods are made. It can also be a place where natural resources are changed into new materials, eg an aluminium smelting works.

Farm – an area of land used for growing crops and/or raising animals.

Field – an area of land cleared of natural vegetation and used to grow crops or raise animals.

Forest – a large and continuous area of land containing growing trees. These can be either natural vegetation or planned by people.

Fossil fuels – fuel produced from fossilised organic material: coal, gas, peat and oil.

Front – the boundary between cold and warm air masses in the atmosphere.

Garden city – a carefully planned town or city where the quality of the environment takes priority in the design, eg Welwyn Garden City.

Gentrification – the process of higher income/professional people moving into an area of a town or city previously seen as a poorer economic area.

Green village – a village that has grown up around an area of land once used for grazing animals.

Greenwich meridian – an imaginary line of longitude, drawn from the north to the south pole, which passes through Greenwich in London.

Grid references – (see pages 22–23)

Habitat – a particular natural or physical environment where a plant or animal will be found.

Hamlet – a small group of buildings in a rural area.

Harbour – a natural or artificially built area of coast that is protected from the sea.

Hemisphere – the northern hemisphere is all the surface of the Earth north of the equator; the southern hemisphere is all the surface south of the equator.

Hurricane – a cyclonic storm in the tropics with winds of more than 120km/h.

Hydrological cycle – the movement of water between sea, land and air.

Hypermarket – a shopping area selling a wide variety of goods, often located on the edge of a town or city, which attracts motorised shoppers.

Immigration – the movement of people into a country with the intention of staying there.

Industry – any business activity. There are many types:
- manufacturing – where goods are produced
- cottage – small-scale making of goods, eg an individual potter
- service – eg an insurance business

- extractive – quarrying and mining
- growth – often using new technology, eg website design
and management.

Infant mortality   the number of deaths per 1000 people of children who die before their first birthday.

Key – explains what all the symbols used on a plan or map mean.

Land use – maps and plans often show what the land is used for.
Latitude – the angular distance of a place north or south of the equator.
Longitude – the angular distance of a place east or west of the Greenwich meridian.
Longshore drift – the gradual movement of particles along a beach as they are carried by the sea's swash and backwash.

Migration – the movement of people around the world.
Modified Mercalli Intensity Scale – a means of allowing earthquake eyewitnesses to use their observations to say how strong an earthquake was.
Moor – unenclosed land, often at high altitude, covered in heather and scrub.

New town – a town or city newly built on open countryside.
Nomads – peoples who don't live in one place, but move around to find food and livestock pastures.
North and south poles – imaginary points around which the Earth spins.

Plate tectonics – the theory used to explain how parts of the Earth's crust move.
Points of the compass – north, south, east, west, etc.
Pollutants – materials that degrade the environment and have harmful effects.
Port – a coastal place where land and sea transport meet.

Quarry – an area of land opened up to extract rock, sand and gravel.

Raw materials – natural materials taken from the environment for human use, eg stone, gas, timber, iron ore.
Recycling – the reusing of waste materials. It reduces the amount of materials dumped and can provide a profit.
Refugee – a person who leaves their country to avoid persecution.

r–w

Residential zone – a place mainly used for people to live in.

Resort – a built-up area used mainly for tourism.

Retailing – the selling of goods and services. It takes many forms, eg large shopping centres, corner shops, internet shopping and mail order.

Scale – controls how much land is represented on a plan or map.

Soil horizon – a soil profile normally contains three horizons. The A horizon may be considered the topsoil. The B horizon is material that is undergoing change through various processes. The C horizon is broken up material made from the bedrock.

Soil profile – a vertical cross-section of soil.

Spit – a shingle or sand beach extending into the sea and linked to land at one end.

Sustainable development – the process by which current levels of exploitation are carefully managed to ensure future generations will be able to meet their needs.

Swash – the movement of water up a beach.

Symbols – used on maps and plans to represent features in the landscape.

The tropics – parts of the Earth's surface up to 23°27' north and south of the equator.

Tides – regular movements of the surface of seas caused by the gravitational pull of the Sun and the Moon.

Transport – the movement of people and goods between places.

Tsunami – huge waves in the oceans caused by tides and earthquakes.

Urban area – a built-up area with a wide range of activities and facilities.

Urbanisation – the spread of towns and cities as they become bigger and take up land previously used for agriculture, and other open spaces.

Velocity – the speed at which a wave travels.

Village – a small rural settlement.

Weather – what is happening in the atmosphere at a given place and time.

Wood – an area of land containing trees growing naturally together.

Index

agriculture 155–6
aid 64–5
analysing evidence 26–8
aspect 82
atlases 19–20, 25, 38
atmosphere 79, 81, 117–8,
    122
autotrophs 83, 85
axis 22

biodiversity 84–5

case studies, fieldwork 174–6
CBDs (central business
    districts) 57, 61
CFCs (chlorofluorocarbons)
    117–8, 122, 126
changes
    global environment 116–23
local environment 111–16
chlorofluorocarbons
    (see CFCs)
cities 56–60, 92–3, 120–1
citizenship 130, 160, 166, 171,
    175–6
climate 14, 78–83, 96
climate change 116–17
coastline processes 145–53
coasts 145–53
    deposition 145, 146
    erosion 147–8, 152, 153,
    157
    human effects 154–8
    models 153
    tourism 156–7

collecting data 18–22, 25–6
community 125
commuters 54
compass points 24
conclusions, drawing 26–8
consumers 29, 83–4
continents 22, 25, 99
contrasting localities 50–2, 95
conurbations 15
counter-urbanisation 57, 61,
    121
County Durham 53, 155
crops 22

data collection 18–21, 25–6
decision-making 35–7
deforestation 76, 117, 119–20,
    122
deposition
    coasts 146
    rivers 136, 139–40, 143–5,
    157
desertification 117, 122
development 63
    sustainable 54, 93, 124–30
digital cameras 179–80, 183
dispersed settlements 53
drainage basins 135–8, 141
drainage patterns 143–5

earthquakes 87, 89, 101–2,
    103–4
eco town 60, 61, 91
ecosystems 83–6, 125
email 178–9

Index

enquiry, geographical 8–12, 13–15, 36
environmental change 111–23
environmental education 110, 127, 129–30
environmental quality 175
equator 20, 22
equity concerns 126
erosion 13, 76, 157
  coasts 147–8, 152–3
  rivers 138–40
European dimension 66–69
eutrophication 156, 157
evidence
  analysing 26–8
  collecting 18–21, 25–6

factories 15
farming 53, 155–6
field sketches 21
fieldwork 132, 160–2, 165
  case studies 174–6
  health and safety issues 34, 158, 164, 168–70
  planning 170–2
  reports 33
  techniques 33–4
  types 162–5
  virtual 177–82
fishing 154
food chains 83–6
food webs 83–4

gentrification 57
geographical enquiry 5, 8–12, 15–18, 36
geographical language 13–15, 22, 30, 166
geographical questions 8–12, 15–18, 19, 36
geographical vocabulary 13–14, 22, 30, 166
geography, teaching 5–6
global alliances 126

global environmental change 116–23
global warming 86, 87, 117, 122, 151
globes 19–20, 22, 39
Greeenwich meridian 22
green villages 54
greenhouse effect 80, 82
grid references 21, 22–3, 25

hamlets 15
health and safety issues 33–4, 158, 164, 168–70
hemisphere 20, 22, 25
human activity 75–6
hurricanes 77, 81
hypermarkets 55

ICT 26, 50, 69, 176, 178–81
  for data collection 26, 175
  and employment 76, 94, 96
  resources 39
industry, coastal 155
inner-city areas 59, 93
issues 29
  (see also decision-making; environmental change; sustainable development)

jigsaw enquiries 174, 176

key questions 11, 15–18
keys 21, 23, 47, 166

land use 12, 21, 24, 46, 50, 53, 59, 95–9, 113, 164, 166, 175
land use surveys 175
language, geographical 13–15, 22, 30, 166
latitude 22, 25, 80
less economically developed countries 63–6
links with other schools 66, 68–9

literacy 32, 33, 177
loads, rivers 137–8, 145
local environmental change
    111–16
local knowledge 28, 37, 90
local resources 12, 45, 49, 56
localities 42–6
    contrasting 50–3, 95
    school 45–8, 95
    urban 61–2
location 40, 96–7
long profiles 136–7
longitude 22, 25
longshore drift 146, 152

maps 19–20, 21, 22–5, 39
meandering 139–40, 141
migration 87–88, 89, 90, 119,
    122
models 77–8
    cities 92–3
    coasts 153
    rain 153
    rivers 77, 143–5, 153
Modified Mercalli Scale 101

natural hazards 81, 83, 87, 88,
    89, 100–2, 117
new technology 76, 94, 96, 97
new towns 28, 60, 96
north and south poles 22
nutrient cycles 84, 85

observation 19
ozone layer 117–18, 122

patterns 71–5, 78, 165
photographs 39, 69
places 41, 44
    European 66–9
    rural 52–6
    urban 56–60
planning fieldwork 170–2
plans 21, 22–5

plate tectonics 99–104
points of the compass 13, 24
pollutants 112, 113
pollution 112, 113, 155, 156
population 87–90, 118–19
presenting information 31–3
process 76
processes 75–8, 165
PSHE 130, 171
push-pull factors 54

quarries 53
questions, geographical 7–12,
    15–18, 19, 36

rain, modelling 153
rainforests 127
RE 175
re-urbanisation 57
recording observations 21
recreation 156–7, 158
    (see also tourism)
refugees 14
residential zones 57
resources 125, 126, 153
resources (teaching)
    (see also virtual fieldwork)
    environmental change
        114–15, 123, 131
    fieldwork 182–3
    geographical enquiry and
        skills 12, 25, 38–9
    ICT 39
    local 12, 45, 49, 56, 62
    patterns and processes 74,
        99, 108–09
    places 45, 49, 50, 51, 62,
        69–70
    sustainable development
        131
    water 143–5, 153, 159
Richter Scale 101
risk assessment 169–70, 174
river channels 137–8

Index

river processes 134–45
river systems 134
rivers 71–2, 77–78
    deposition 139–40, 143–5
    erosion 138–40
    loads 137–8, 145
    long profiles 136–7
    models 77, 143–5, 153
    underground 140–1
rocky shores 150
rural change 54–5
rural deprivation 55
rural mosaic 55
rural places 52–6
rural settlements 52–6, 90–2, 94

safety 33–4, 158 164
sand dunes 150
sand trays 78, 143–5, 153
scale 19, 21, 24
school buildings 46–7
school grounds 47
school links 66, 68–9, 95, 158
school localities 45–8, 95
sea level changes 151
secondary sources 20–1
sediment 135, 137–8, 140, 141, 143–5
seismometers 102, 103
sense of place 41
settlements 52–6, 59–60, 90–5
    (see also cities)
sites 40
soil horizons 107, 108
soil profiles 107, 108
soils 106–8
sources, secondary 20–1
street names 12, 95
street patterns 72–3
suburbs 59, 61, 93
succession 84, 85

sustainable development 65, 93, 124–30
symbols 19, 21, 23, 24, 47, 166

teachers' roles 163–4, 165
teaching primary geography 5–6
technological change 96
tides 15, 147, 152
tornadoes 81, 82
tourism 76, 77
towns
    (see cities; urban places)
transport 12, 111–12, 125–6
tropics 22
tsunami 88, 102

underground rivers 140–1
urban deprivation 59, 61
urban places 56–60
urban settlements 92–3, 94
    (see also cities; towns)
urbanisation 57–9, 61, 120–1, 122, 154–5

vicinity 49
video cameras 179–80, 183
views (opinions) 29, 35–7
villages 15, 53–4
virtual fieldwork 177–82
visits 66, 158, 160–2
    (see also fieldwork)
vocabulary, geographical 13–15, 22, 30, 166
volcanoes 87, 88, 100, 103

waste disposal 112, 113, 115–16
water cycle 79, 133–4
water flow 137–8
waves 146
weather 75, 78–83
weathering 104–6, 148
woodland 53